The Golden Flower

The Golden Flower

Toltec Mastery of Dreaming and Astral Voyaging

by Koyote the Blind

Gateways Books & Tapes
Nevada City, California
2018

The Golden Flower
Toltec Mastery of Dreaming and Astral Voyaging
© copyright 2018 by Koyote the Blind (Ricardo Flores)
First Trade Edition
Cover art by Sharla Sanchez
Cover design by Gailyn Porter
Layout by Gailyn Porter
Editing by Iven Lourie

Trade Paperback ISBN: 978-0-89556-613-3
Kindle ISBN: 978-0-89556-280-7
PDF ISBN: 978-0-89556-614-0
MobiPocket ISBN: 978-0-89556-616-4
EPUB ISBN: 978-0-89556-617-1

Published by:
Gateways Books & Tapes / I.D.H.H.B., Inc.
P.O. Box 370
Nevada City, California 95959
(530) 271-2239
info@gatewaysbooksandtapes.com

Library of Congress Cataloging-in-Publication Data

Names: Koyote, the Blind, 1965- author.
Title: The golden flower : the Toltec mastery of dreaming and astral
voyaging
    / by Koyote the Blind.
Description: First [edition].. | Nevada City, California :
    Gateways-I.D.H.H.B., Inc., 2018. | Previously published under title: The
    golden flower : the yoga of dreaming and astral mastery.
Identifiers: LCCN 2018007619 (print) | LCCN 2018019402 (ebook) |
ISBN
    9780895566133 (trade pbk.) | ISBN 9780895566140 (Pdf) | ISBN
9780895566164 (
    Mobi-pocket) | ISBN 9780895566171 (Epub) | ISBN 9780895562807
(Kindle)
Subjects: LCSH: Dreams. | Astral projection. | Toltecs--Miscellanea.
Classification: LCC BF1078 (ebook) | LCC BF1078 .K69 2018 (print) |
DDC
    135/.3--dc23
LC record available at https://lccn.loc.gov/2018007619

THIS BOOK IS DEDICATED TO BRAHMA,
THE ONE WHO SLEEPS IN THE PALACE WHERE
THE ETERNAL RESIDENT WHO READS THIS BOOK
MOVES FROM DREAM TO DREAM...

A Voyager Has Come This Way

a voyager has come this way
stalking wild places
far and near,
he has given us
more than a glimpse,
from his open mouth
an outpouring of winged words
have filled us
with an unexpected hope
and a discovery of places
that even our dreams
had not suspected,
words carried to the skies,
plunging to the depths
like mysterious creatures
dwelling in the ocean deep,
breathe pure spirit
from the very inside of life,
our eyes have been opened,
rendering retreat impossible,
carried by sounds
born of these places
we find and unlock as we sojourn,
the many chambers,
secret to the profane,
steeped in the mysteries,
each with a different
and indecipherable face

in the house of many mansions,
it is here that we discover
who we have always been,
each step bringing us
simultaneously inside and outside,
revealing to ourselves
just how big we are,
setting the heart free
to weave a soul
that fills the whole world,
teaching us what it means
to be a voyager,
and walk with the one called
Koyote.

Gerald Porter

Also by Koyote the Blind:

Teachings of a Toltec Survivor
This book contains Koyote's lectures given during a three month course on Toltec wisdom and esoteric teachings. These chapters carry the unique space he created for the students taking the course, and you get the unmistakable feeling of being present as you bathe in the radiations of the Teaching Chamber.

Adumbrations
A pocket book of haiku with an intriguing and erudite introduction by the author on the subject.

Tolteca I, II, and III
A journal of articles by Koyote on Toltec history, philosophy, esoteric wisdom, and art. Only three of nine issues have been released.

Teomoxtli
This is a subscription course with weekly monographs created to transmit the theoretical and practical knowledge of the Toltec's "book of divinity," a fountain of information and techniques from the original western tradition of the Toltecs.

For information on courses and seminars taught by Koyote, as well as performances of The Telling, check out our website: www.koyotetheblind.com

Check out Koyote's titles on his Amazon Author's Page: www.amazon.com/author/koyote

Follow him on Facebook in "The Telling by Koyote the Blind" page: www.facebook.com/koyotetheblind/

Table of Contents

Acknowledgments

My deepest gratitude for all those who collaborated in the creation of this book through their work, their teachings, their encouragement, their financial support, their artistic gifts, and, above all, their aspirations:

To my father, the Salvadorian poet Ricardo Arcadio Flores, who early on taught me to pray, then to observe myself, and then to free myself from all dreams.
Without this tireless grounding in questioning and silence, no mastery is possible.

To my mother, Jilma Lilian Flores, whose voice exhorted me every night of my childhood to sleep with the angels.

To Francis Fanci, an amazing magician and devoted teacher, who held my hand as a young teenager and led me to an amazing world. With him, I witnessed the opening of the veil and swam in the mystical waters of Siloam, the boundless light. He helped me see that no ability is worthwhile if it is not used to serve.

To Father Ignacio Knörr, my Jesuit mentor, who taught me that every dream and every experience is a dialogue with God.

To Don Florentino, who showed me that all I needed was already inside me, and who spoke so clearly in the eternal language of the real.

To Eric Kauffman, who taught me the importance of keeping a dream journal; and to Rey De Lupos, who brought home this valuable lesson and turned it into a lifelong habit.

To Baba Hari Dass, who revealed the mystery of the dreamer absolute, Brahman, the sleeper of the palace who dreams the dream of the King of the palace: the ever present Jivah, the eternal unborn.

To Tezaqui Güitame Cachora, my beloved benefactor, who guided me as gently and as harshly as needed through the voyages to higher planes, to the knowledge and conversation of the residents of the spirit world, and to the ultimate initiation, the communion with the source of all magick and all goodness.

To E.J. Gold, a true teacher of teachers. E.J. has always been a teacher of means, creating tools and guiding into what would otherwise seem impossible feats. His example and encouragement in the pursuit of this Great Work for the benefit of All Beings Everywhere will forever be present in the macro-dimensions for all seekers. I also thank him for writing such a beautiful and touching foreword, and for being a great friend and mentor to my community.

To the unknown young man who, during a massacre when we all thought we would die, showed me in no uncertain terms that this too was a dream and that I could face that moment as I faced life: by taking responsibility for my experience and transform the dream into a sacred moment.

To my daughter, Xochitl, a beautiful dreamer who created the art piece used on the cover of this book.

To my son, Alec, who always brings me games and stories that stimulate my engagement with the Dreaming.

To Sharla Sanchez, who designed the cover art. Sharla also developed a technique for building the Dream Altar that effectively channels the power and presence of the moon. She teaches this technique in weekend workshops. Sharla also conducts dream circles.

To Carlos Flores, my brother and first student. He has been an avid and dedicated seeker since, as a little boy, he asked for these teachings. He led the team of editors who patiently perused this book and constantly challenged me to say what I wanted to say better. His explorations of the Dreaming have awakened a devotional practice and service to others through an oracle.

To Kristin Harris, a powerful dreamer who also conducts her own dream circles, which include teachings from my own benefactor, Cachora. Kristin also served as editor of this book.

To I.D.H.H.B. for giving permission to use E.J. Gold's illustration of The Seven Bodies of Man.

To Gerald Porter, for the beautiful poem, *A Voyager Has Come This Way.*

To those whose generosity made this book a reality. Without them, this book would not have journeyed from the womb of the unconscious to your hands. Especially deserving of mention for their invaluable financial contribution:

Pablo Abbona, Loria Anthony Andrew Bishop, Gregory Bucy, Season Cole, Eric de la Parra, Sylvia Yunuen Diego, Thomas Eric Dietzel, Carlos Flores, Diana Flores, David Franco, Pilar Gamboa, Kristin Harris, Jim Hodgkinson, David Humphries, Maurice Laflamme, Francisco Maioli, Tim Newbury, Gerald and Gailyn Porter, George Ramos, Roberta Ma Satya, Nam Kaur Romm, Crystal Sanchez, Samira Sekhon, Jordan Scott Tesch, Brandi Thomas.

Finally, I want to thank my spiritual family, the dream yogins whose aspiration and dedication make the teachings not only a possibility, but an imperative. They have gone beyond merely applying my teachings to developed practices of their own. Dream circles, vision-quests, sweat lodges, dream altar creations, dream catcher creations and workshops, divination practices, and story-telling are just some of the artistic and spiritual practices being developed by advanced practitioners. They are helping in taking the teachings beyond where they found them, internalizing and making them their own. Without you all, nothing I do would have any value.

Foreword

I've been reading Koyote's new book on dreaming and astral voyaging. Dreaming is a great key to astral voyaging, soul questing and sky walking in general. When you're dreaming, the body is asleep, passive and largely motor-reflexive, but the attention is still active, passing from one reality set to another, which opens the door to astral travel.

The body has reactions to astral travel, and it's best to keep it in a relaxed and passive state, so it won't interfere with the process. There is a connection between your spirit and your body, which is eternal and is present during the body's entire lifetime, and it is that connection which pulls you back when there is a disturbance near the body or the body is uncomfortable or distressed.

Dreaming is the Great Key, and Koyote's lessons in flying will take you there. I recommend this book highly, and will suggest it to anyone who asks me a question on the subject— his answers and mine will be the same.

Thank you, Koyote, for your well-written and well- conceived contribution to the Great Work.

See You At The Top!!!

E.J. Gold

Preface

The dream world was strongly present for me when I was just a baby, and one could say that it has always been as real for me as the physical reality of the waking. Early on, I trained myself to explore the Dreaming and my own limits. I learned to awaken within the dream and, in that lucid state, to dare to the limits of my imagination to experience and perform anything and everything. I trained myself to face all my fears, and this attitude helped me face a physical reality at times laden with dangers, with horrors even. Yet, the beauty I found in my dreaming experiments also helped me find astonishing beauty in my life.

As portentous and glorious as the dreaming landscape of my childhood was, the most enriching results came from testing myself to the limits. The experiences in the Dreaming were not as much about what I could experience as it was about exploring myself, the limits of my own fears, the nature of my own consciousness, and ultimately, the truth about my Self.

At some point in life, learning to dream became identical to learning to live. The teachers I was fortunate to meet were impeccable guides in both realms, and with maturity and understanding, I came to see that the experiences in the waking and in the Dreaming were actually the same, that it was always I experiencing an environment. I began to realize that there were two halves of me, one who was the dreamer and one who was the avatar created in each dream. I came to realize that the personality I had developed to navigate the waking world was just another avatar, no different than the ones created to navigate the Dreaming and the higher planes of consciousness. I was living many lives, and I was becoming increasingly conscious that I always existed in many planes and that existence itself follows the nature of dreaming. At this point, I decided to explore the worlds beyond my own imagination and dreaming, seeking to experience those realms existing beyond the limits of my own physical body.

Around the age of twelve, I started trying to come out of my body and know the world and know the astral plane. I had a hard time accomplishing this properly. I tried for years, practice after practice, until at the age of sixteen, I had success in that area; and since then, I have been exploring the Dreaming and the other planes.

Later, at the age of 30, I met my benefactor, a Yaqui-Lacandon Nahual who taught me all kinds of techniques and gave me much experience in voyaging through the planes. He took my raw talent and tested it to the limits, triggering inner knowledge and access to gnosis. He showed me how to contact the source of all power and all knowledge, and in this endeavor, I mastered the art of dreaming and the secrets of flying through the higher planes of existence.

After teaching a close group of students this ancient art, I have been asked many times to put my knowledge and experiences in writing. This is how this book was conceived. It is a manual on the art of dreaming and the mastery of the astral plane. More than that, it is a tome on the Yoga of Dreaming, the attainment through dreaming. I am calling this book The Golden Flower because of the nature of the essence behind all experience and all dreaming. The chapter found in Part III under the same name describes this experience faithfully.

This book contains an account of my experiences and exercises, and the knowledge that was passed down to me through a Toltec shamanic lineage, through the mystery schools of the west, and through the Tantrica lineage into which I was also initiated. This book will contain not only theory, but the practices—the exercises for you to attain mastery in this area. It is the result of 40 years of practice, training and intense work under a Shaivic tantric tradition, a Toltec shamanic lineage, and various esoteric schools of the Western Mysteries.

The Golden Flower is a practical, as well as a scholarly, work delivered in a poetic prose designed to be clear and illuminating to the conscious mind, while triggering an awakening factor in the subconscious mind that will enable the practitioner to achieve high levels of consciousness, maze brightness, and abilities to voyage and experience the higher dimensions. It is much more than an interesting read; it is a tool designed to provide clear and definite abilities and changes in the reader.

You will learn to:

• Dream more vividly and masterfully.

• Use your enhanced dreaming to seek answers, guidance, enjoyment, and breakthroughs in your waking life and spiritual path

• Develop an etheric body with which you can travel anywhere on the face of the world.

• Develop a body of light which can detach fully from the physical body and which can be used to fly to higher planes of existence.

• Awaken the psychic senses to perceive and interact with the infinite, invisible world around.

The information in this book is the result of experience, learning, and experimentation. It also contains proven exercises taught in private sessions, public lectures, and numerous workshops and intensives offered in the past twelve years.

In my interaction with those master dreamers who had been my mentors and teachers, true luminaries in this world and beyond, I learned over and over that the true teachings are not—cannot be— imparted by the rational, ordinary mind alone. Don Florentino always spoke from a place that seemed to resonate within me, as if he was at once speaking from the most intimate silence within myself, as well as from the outskirts of my sense-experience. To listen to him was to partake of his wisdom, and each word was understood in its finer details, as if I had the opportunity to fully ponder on it. Alejandro Jodorowsky showed me the power of oneiric art, the healing and transformative power archetypes have of communicating with the body, and the way to engage in this arcane language of the unconscious through art and performance. E.J. Gold showed me the art and technology of creating sacred spaces, and the ins and outs of taking a group of people and travel across different worlds, dimensions, and timelines. Every time I thought something would be impossible to do, he would show me how to do it, and every visit to him would trigger jumps in the ability to voyage, dream, and transform. Finally, Cachora trained me for two intense years in many shamanic disciplines, and his training was happening simultaneously in the waking and in the Dreaming. It became second nature to see and hear him in both worlds at the same time. To integrate all his teachings and unify these two realms was the conclusion of my training with him.

After my encounters with these men of power and knowledge, it was impossible for me to consider a workshop where I would only explain a few exercises and share concepts about the Dreaming. In each workshop and intensive I offered, I had to do as it had been done to me. I had, in order to pay homage to and honor the teachers who had given so much before me, to do more than just teach the ordinary, rational mind. Instead, I would create a space in the waking, as well as in the Dreaming, a space that would protect and contain the dreamers, where I could guide them in the art of voyaging, of experiencing, and of having an encounter with Power. Each intensive, then, became an extraordinary experience for each participant, where these techniques could be conveyed through actual, unmediated experience. When faced with the possibility of writing this book, I wanted it to be as useful as one-on-one training with me would be. I wanted this book to be much more than an introduction to the ideas and techniques of dreaming. I wanted this book to be a tool and a sacred artifact through which the student can access the higher realms of experience, and through which the Teachings themselves can be accessed.

This book, therefore, has been designed to trigger in the reader the experience of the higher dreaming, astral voyaging, and shadow walking. This book also contains a doorway to the higher initiatory intelligence that guides humanity and which I was fortunate enough to have encountered in the higher planes, as well as in the flesh of impeccable teachers.

I believe that humans are free to roam about this Earth in their physical bodies, in their astral bodies, in their etheric form, to change and shape and shift as they will, and to fly into the higher planes of existence—to learn, to grow and to evolve spiritually. The Golden Flower is in itself an artifact that will trigger these experiences for you. Reading it will be an act, magical and sacred, and it will teach you in practical ways and in experiential ways. Help me in my task of offering these Teachings to the world by practicing these techniques and by mastering your dreaming. It's a good thing for the world to see these Teachings at this time.

To obtain the full benefits of this book, I encourage you to read it from cover to cover once, performing any exercises and experiments that appeal to you. Then, go back to any chapters that draw you in, paying closer attention to their teachings and experiments. After a little while, you will notice a dramatic change in your dreams. You should keep a dream journal, and when you notice your dreaming is changing, go back to read the book. You will then notice many things you missed the first time.

The book is divided into three parts. The first part contains theory and exercises designed to help you explore the Dreaming and master yourself in any dream. The second part presupposes some familiarity with the Dreaming and leads the reader to become acquainted and, eventually, master the ability to move beyond the confines of the physical body and fly to the higher planes of existence. It is in these levels that consciousness begins to experience a life eternal and beyond the confines of the human form. The third part is a collection of higher level teachings. They are initiatory Tellings, and reading them aloud or in meditative silence will trigger in you the knowledge held in the recesses of your flesh and experiences carried by your spirit throughout the many sojourns through innumerable incarnations. Read these chapters in the third part with full attention and without distractions. Read every word as if it is a world unto itself. Feel the reverberations of each word, regardless of the understanding of your limited thinking mind. The reading itself will trigger in you initiatory experiences.

At some point, if you take these teachings to heart, you will find that this book is a true artifact through which you can access higher knowledge of how to dream, how to live, how to die, and how to attain freedom.

Introduction

What is a dream?

It is a passage between a pregnant silence and the prelude to dawn.

What then, is a dream?

It is the totality of experience, the unity of the being and the non-being.

It is the non-linear perception of the vast mystery.

A dream is what we truly are in the face of the immensity of the void.

It is a lifetime, the island of existence in an ocean of eternity.

A dream is the point of view the dreamer creates in its communion with Self.

Every night we face death; the dissolution of identity as we let go of the need to be; and every night we create ourselves out of the mystery of death, finding ourselves in the midst of an environment we call *dream* when we wake up. Yet, this dream we call *reality* as we are going through it. A dream then is the remembered reality we left behind. A reality is but the dream we are currently experiencing.

Every dream emerges out of the vast darkness of consciousness we know as the One Who Sleeps: a consciousness without beginning or end, without identity or point of view. It emerges without knowing how, created in the mysterious womb of the Mother, animated with a purpose it does not comprehend, even as it embodies said purpose. The dream self thus created is imbued with the seed purpose of the Father, that hidden purpose that emerges out of the will of the vast selfless consciousness of the One Who

Sleeps—who is called Dreamer when it dreams, but is No One in the depth of the sleep beyond the dream and the wake.

What is the Dreaming?

It is a palace created from all the possible experiences to be had by All Beings Everywhere. The Dreamer is the resident of the Palace. The True Self is the hidden one who sleeps. The sleeper is the dreamer who dreams, hidden and unseen, unaffected and of a different order of reality. The sleeper in the Palace is Brahma, Ometeotl, the Absolute. The resident of the Palace is the experiencer, the voyager, Hadit, Atman.

You are the totality of it all. You are the hidden source of all experience, the experiencer, and the environment we call the Dreaming.

What is the Dreaming?

It is the totality of all possible experiences, and to master the art of dreaming is to master the art of living, of existence. It is to master oneself in its most true form. For a dream is not only what happens at night when you rest, it is in fact that which you experience at any level of consciousness. Whether a dog or a god, you are in fact always a center of experience experiencing a dream. Learn to master your dreaming. This is accomplished by learning to master yourself as you dream, mastering your perceptions and your intent.

Such is the intent of this book, to lead you step by step at all levels of your being, to acquire the essential and eternal habit of knowing you are in a dream, of remembering yourself as the dreamer, and of mastering your perceptions to consciously engage with the dream.

There are two possible ways of consciously engaging with the dream:

1. You can experience it and, like a gamer, carry out your intent within it: accomplishing missions, attaining, fighting, navigating,

meeting characters, etc. In other words, in every dream, as in every game, you can experience it, learn from it; and above all, you can do your will by applying your abilities and *ingenium* to the nature of the environment, and in this way seek to accomplish your pure will.

2. You can wake up.

You can adjust the intensity of your experience. Everything that exists follows the laws of vibration, polarity, and rhythm. Everything that can be perceived or measured in any way is subject to these principles. Therefore, the dreamer can learn to upscale or downscale its own perception, which is to say that you can take on more or less information. It is like adjusting the lens of your consciousness by manipulating your attention.

You can upscale to move to a higher scale of vibration, which in effect changes the environment you find yourself in. This is a higher level shamanic technique, but quite easy to perform once you get the hang of it. Upscaling and downscaling is how a shaman moves between planes of existence, shape-shifts, and learns to access information seemingly unavailable to others.

Following the principles taught in this book, we can learn to engage existence with greater degrees of mastery, until there comes a point when we become masters of our own experience. This is magick, defined by Aleister Crowley as "causing change to occur in conformity with Will."[1] Understanding the principles of dreaming implies understanding the laws of the universe; and to control the experience we have, means to control our perceptions. Towards this mastery over the Dreaming, is what this book strives for. However, this change in conformity with Will can take an outward or an inward direction.

In any given experience, you can transform the dream (i.e., the outward part of the experience) or the dreamer. This is mastery of

1 Crowley, A. (1997). Magick in theory and practice. In Liber ABA, p. 126.

external magick, of sorcery. It's at the center of "Do what thou wilt" of Thelemic philosophy. You can also transform yourself, which is at the center of all mystical systems and all higher alchemy. In fact, self-transformation is at the hidden core of "Do what thou wilt," for it is the hidden center of one's true nature who truly wills. To do thy will you have to identify with the center of your true nature, and not with the doing of external experience. **It has always been an integral part of the teachings of the Toltecs to learn to go through a dream without changing it, to go through a room without leaving a trace, to become invisible and unimportant.** Why? Precisely because there is a time when it is important in one's training to guide the intent and all of one's resources into the inner transformation of one's consciousness and one's being. All attention, then, is placed in self transformation, leaving the dream to unfold as it should. This is the esoteric meaning of "let the dead bury the dead," uttered by Jesus to the man who wanted to delay his spiritual work until he had buried his parents.

Of course, in practice, it is rarely the case that the change is unilateral. Changes in our external circumstance can lead to insights and changes inside of us; and transformation of who we are, or even how we see ourselves, can lead to changes in the world that surrounds us. The master dreamer must therefore learn to balance the outer and the inner, equally able to master the dream as well as the self, and in fact, creating synergy between both so that one initiates the other and vice versa. The changes of consciousness trigger changes in one's sphere of influence, and the rearrangement of external conditions lead to inner changes.

In all cases, the work of mastering the Dreaming is both internal and external, in increasing degrees of subtlety and granularity, until we acquire the essential and eternal habit of becoming conscious.

It should be clear by now that this book is not only about the dream we have when in horizontal sleep. It is also about the dream we have any time we are having any experience, from the dreams where the unconscious lives and experiences, to the dreams of ordinary life, to the conscious dreams of traveling through the higher planes, to the cosmic dream of the totality of existence itself. This book presents the teaching and practice to gain mastery over the Dreaming at all its levels, and eventually to gain the mastery to awaken.

Beyond any experience whatsoever, there is the waking. There are gradations of waking, from realizing we are dreaming, which implies that we wake up enough to know we are in a dream, to fully leaving the dream, a state belonging to a being for whom existence itself seems as a dream in comparison to the state beyond, the true waking.

Any experience whatsoever is part of a dream, at any level or plane of existence. Above it all, there is the quiet plenitude of the void, the wake world.

This is the book of the waking. It is a complete teaching by the method of experience. It is the basis of Tantra, and the heart of all Yoga. This book is about attaining the waking within any dream, and beyond the Dreaming and the wakeful state waits the Golden Flower of the Garden of the House Absolute.

Angel's Orb
Sharla Sanchez

Part One

In the Garden of Dreams Grows the Flower of Experience

Fearless

I started working in the Dreaming when I was very young. I was a little four-year-old boy in El Salvador. I was having disturbing recurring dreams where I died. In the dream, I would fly; and the flying brought tremendous pleasure, but a self-defeating thought would come each time. It was the thought that I would fall. Was that thought there because I felt the tensions and overheard the talks all around me of the social injustices and military repression that seemed to be boiling to the point of inevitable war? Was it the lingering memories of my birth, when I found myself flying free in the higher aethers in between incarnations, only to see myself making a wrong move of my attention that would make me fall and get trapped in an organic matrix of electrical energy called *the human nervous system*? It could be a collaboration of factors, but at the time, I was simply feeling overwhelmed by these dreams. **The initial flying felt like freedom and power, but the thought of falling would come, and as it is wont in the Dreaming, a thought is a directional command.** Each time, I would fall, and the fall came with dread. I would then wake up before hitting the floor, sweating and trembling, my heart palpitating.

My senses became very open at that time. I started seeing the invisible world around me and, without anyone to really guide me through that, I was filled with panic and dread. I started fearing death, imagining my body decomposing and being devoured by worms. The darkness would arrive with the sounds of the tropical night, and I would lie in bed with my senses open and my nervous system lit. I started seeing spirits and creatures invisible to others. It only increased my fear at night, seeing the elemental spirits surrounding me. In my childish imagination, I thought I saw witches around

3

my bed, whispering incantations and changing their faces into any horrific vision that my imagination would invoke.

At some point, this recurring dream started to happen. I would walk this path that led away from my home and a witch would come out of a neighbor's house. She was crazy, screaming at the top of her lungs, laughing; and her laughter seemed to penetrate my skull. I would start running around an almond tree in front of her house—just running around in circles. She would keep following me with her crazy laughter, until she would catch me and stab me with her knife.

Every time this would happen, I would awaken in panic. Until one day, I found myself in a dream under the shade of that almond tree. A young man was there, sitting by the tree, and I next to him. He asked me why I was afraid of dying. We spoke at length in this dream. **After a while, he told me that there was no place called** ***death*****, but only sleeping, dreaming, and waking. "You are only scared because you don't know how to wake up,"** he said. "I'll teach you how to wake up." With that promise, he closed his eyes, grabbed his eyelids with his delicate fingers, and opened them. I followed his example; and grabbing my eyelids, I opened my eyes and woke up. I felt excited, thinking I had just learned a big secret. I knew how to wake up from any dream!

I immediately went back to sleep, and I found myself walking up the street from my house; and when I passed by the almond tree, I could sense the presence behind the door—the dreaded presence of the witch. Like always, she dashed out with her long face with six eyes and her hideous laughter. In panic, I started running around the tree, but this time, I had a secret. I grabbed my eyelids and opened them, finding myself in my bed, not sweating nor trembling. I was happy and elated. Enthusiastically, I went back into the dream. I found myself again in front of the almond tree. The witch didn't come out. My mind calm, I found out that it was I who called her out with my fearful anticipation. With my mind quiet, I knew she was behind the dark doorway, but held her there with my silence. I decided then to fly. I flew. Higher and higher, I went. I held the thought of falling back with my silence, and the fear of falling stayed in the shadows of my subconscious, like the witch behind the doorway by the almond tree. I flew and landed.

This event started a bold series of experiments in the Dreaming. I shape-shifted, grew tall like a giant to explore vast lands and cross oceans, bigger still, to see galaxies dancing in my hands. I became eagle and whale, cat and shadow. I went to deserts and jungles. I talked to masters and discarnate beings. **Over the decades, I exercised the limits of my imagination, knowing that I could roam the entirety of creation without fear. I had a secret: I could wake up at will.**

At one point, however, I realized that the limits of my experiences were still confined by the fear of dying. I decided to experience this passage in the dream, encouraged by the words of that young man who assured there was no death, just the passage between dreams, the sleep, and the waking.

One day, I became lucid in a dream and, fully aware that I was dreaming, I decided to fly. I flew, and this time I allowed the thought of falling to bubble up from the shadows of my unconscious. I fell. I held in check the desire to open my eyes and wake up. I felt the impact on the floor, and died. The superstitions of many had told me that if you die in a dream, you die for real. I didn't die a physical death. Instead, I found myself in a field of light without forms, vast and musical. It was an indescribable experience, and my child's mind was unable to fully explain it or classify it.

Encouraged by the success of my experiments in the Dreaming, I decided to revisit my fear laden limits. One day, I found myself standing by the almond tree. I called the witch out of the shadows, and I ran around the tree to follow protocol. This time, I ran without fear. I decided to let it happen. I allowed her to come out. I allowed her to stab me; and I allowed myself to die; and when I died, her laughter started ringing off like tiny bells in the distance; and somehow I knew, I remembered, that I had been there already. Then, I woke up inside another space, another dream; and in this dream, I was sitting by a tree and a tiger came and devoured me. I allowed him to devour me. I felt his teeth entering my flesh and tearing me apart, and I died. I went dream after dream dying in many ways.

I woke up knowing that there was something in this dream world that needed to be explored or understood. And then, with great enthusiasm, I started going into the Dreaming, exploring things, flying, becoming as big as a galaxy, becoming small like an ant— smaller than that, like a molecule ... smaller than an atom. I would travel and move, change my face, change my shape and so on. I learned much, and the guides in the Dreaming started guiding me, telling me where to go, what to do, and how to experience different things.

I encourage you earnestly to be fearless in your experimentation. Create the habit of going beyond the limits of your fear. The key is to know that nothing can really happen to you, no matter what happens to your dream avatar. Nothing and no one can harm you. You cannot truly harm anyone in the dream. Even if attacked, hurt, and killed, you will wake up unharmed, alive, and intact. If you offend someone you love, kill someone, or burn your house, you will wake up and no one will feel offended, no one will have been killed by you, and your house will still be standing. **There is no guilt in a dream; feel free, therefore, to do as you will.**

Of course, one could say that this admonition only works if you are lucid, knowing that you are dreaming. This is only partly true. On the one hand, even if we become lucid during a dream, we might still be ridden by fear and guilt, and that will stop us from going beyond the limits of our habitual dreaming. On the other hand, even if we don't know we are dreaming, we benefit from being able to think beyond the limits of our fears. Therefore, training ourselves to go beyond our fears is something useful in itself.

Developing the ability to become lucid is of tremendous help for all work in the Dreaming. The next chapter will provide clear and useful training for developing lucidity and for remembering your dreams. However, you do not need to wait until you can become lucid in your dreams to do these experiments. In fact, it is very important to develop the habit of experimenting, regardless of whether you are lucid or not. Practice outside your dreams and you will train your unconscious to practice any time.

ॐॐॐॐ

This is the trick: use your imagination to perform these experiments. You do not need to be sleeping to perform them. Relax your body and clear your mind by using any relaxation or meditation technique you know. Lie down in a calm and comfortable place where you can be free of interruptions and distractions. Close your eyes and imagine yourself in a safe and pleasant place. Now, imagine a dream where you experience whatever you want to experience. Face your fears knowing you can wake up any time. Here, you can:

• Experience many deaths and many rebirths.
• Grow as tall as you want, as tall as the Galaxy. Grow until the entire universe is just a particle inside you and, therefore, you are nowhere in creation.
• Grow as small as an ant, or a molecule, or an atom. Keep going until subatomic particles seem as big as worlds.
• Become a member of the opposite gender. Experience this new body.
• Become different animals; smell, see, hear, and move as they do. Feel their hunger and hunt.
• Be the wind, fire, a storm.
• Be an inanimate object. Feel what that is like.
• Experience walking through walls, swimming in the asphalt, and being invisible.
• Become various beings of non-human forms.
• Talk to people you know, and people you wish you knew. Hold entire conversations with them.

CB&)CR&)

The only limits to what we can be or what we can experience are in our own imagination. We tend to stop ourselves from new experiences, more out of habit than out of fear. There is a habit of the mind to think of ourselves as limited and constricted to our physical form. Because we think we are our body, we tend to dream as if we had the exact same body and the same gender as when we are awake. That is, we automatically create our dream avatar as a replica of our physical form. Go beyond this tendency when you practice, and practice often!

This practice will transfer to your dreaming and, soon, you will find yourself experiencing these events in your dreams. **It is very important, and I can't stress this point enough, to have a dream journal. Get a journal dedicated to your dreaming and astral projection experiences.** When you do the exercises above, always write down the experiences and sensations you had. We will talk more about the importance of the journal in the next chapter.

One most invaluable technique to be learned and applied in any dream, and in any environment whatsoever, is the ability to remember oneself as the dreamer, so that one can distinguish between the one who dreams and the avatar that has been created in that dream. The effort necessary to remember oneself as a dreamer is the kind of effort that ties a string of memory between one dream and the other. The untrained attention immerses you into the simulation that you are creating in that moment, and when you disengage it to move into another simulation, nothing is threaded from the previous simulation to the new simulation. Nothing is threaded from the world you were in just a moment ago and the world where you find yourself at this very moment. And so you go, from dream to dream, from lifetime to lifetime, from avatar to avatar, from environment to environment, always thinking that this is where you have always been; always thinking that this is who you are; always thinking that this is what happens to you. When you acquire the habit of remembering yourself as the dreamer, you come to know when you are making a switch; you come to know that you have, just now, been somewhere else; and remember, not only where you were, but also the transition.

The technique for remembering yourself is the most simple technique—just a constant mantra, from the simple "I am that I am," to the technique of invoking your presence into the present, to the technique of asking, "Is this a dream?"

A secondary technique which opens many doorways is the technique of challenging the limits of that environment. Whenever you find yourself in a dream, try to bring the experience to its maximum potential. If you can fly in the dream, fly, and go up and up, and see how far you can go. Move up, up, up, up. Don't stop. Keep going. Avoid the temptation of drifting back into sleep, and put all your force into going up. Keep going up until you have exhausted all your force, until you find yourself unable to go up anymore, and then try to go up some more. You'll be surprised by where you wake up, by where you find yourself after such an effort. Alter the size of your body. Become bigger and bigger and bigger, until the planet cannot hold you, and keep growing until the solar system becomes just a spec of light in the center of your heart. Keep growing until the galaxy is the size of your body, and keep growing until all the stars and all galactic clusters have become so small that the entire universe seems to be a vanishing point in the distance, remote and silent within your own body. In another dream, become small. See everything around you doubling in size—the chairs, the people, the walls, everything growing twice its size; and then, twice its size again, so you become smaller and smaller, until you are able to perceive the giant insects; and then, smaller than that, until you perceive the vibrations of the molecules all around you; and smaller than that, where the universe is just a chaotic collection of shimmering points; and then, smaller than that, until every atom becomes as vast and impossible as the universe itself. Change your form; become the opposite gender in your dream; live a dream as the opposite of who you are. Do good. Do evil. Experience pain and suffering. Experience everything you are afraid of. Be devoured by a tiger. Let the jaguar tear off your face. Be buried alive. Drown. Be burned at the stake. Notice your flesh decaying, your bones being gnawed, your body rotting and dissolving, floating in a river. Die a thousand deaths in your dreams. Expose yourself to that. Learn to not awaken when you are about to die. Learn to die, and see that you don't always awaken in your ordinary existence, that sometimes you awaken after death in a higher dimension, in an impossibly alien world. Become an animal, a crow, a cat, a bee. Become an inanimate object in your dreams. Become no one— just a silent observer of the dream. Become the other people that you see in the dream. Put yourself in their perspective, and dream the dream they are dreaming. Walk through walls. Become a cloud. Be the wind that moves the green leaves in the forest.

Experiment in your dreams to the limits of your imagination. Do not believe that your only possible experience is a human experience, and do not believe that the only possible human experience is the experience of your habitual form.

In every dream, you have the entirety of the human experience at your disposal. You can be anyone and anything that your subconscious mind can conceive. You will find in these experiments tremendous power, freedom, and the range of emotions and moods that will give you the experience of millions of lifetimes in one. Practice. Be creative. Be fearless in your dreams. If you are fearless in your dreams, you will find yourself applying the same fearlessness in your life. If you are able to lose your form in your dreams, you will find yourself beyond your ordinary form in your waking life. Eventually, this will lead to that moment in which you are no longer just experiencing the simulation of the reality created within your brain; but you are able to, actually, perceive outside of the simulation, into the actual world; because you will not be perceiving with the senses anymore, but with another body that has become possible through the unification of your waking avatar with

11

your dream avatar. **You'll be able to perceive, then, the objective world and, from there, live a life so difficult to explain, yet so magnificent that any other portion of your ordinary life will pale in comparison—for every experience that you had within this simulation of reality will be duller and more muted than the direct, raw, perception of the light bombarding all the senses of your body in this very moment.**

Live, then, without fear for the ending of the dream. There is no death other than the death of the avatar within a simulation. The fear of death comes from having come to believe that the form of the avatar is your actual reality. These experiments are designed to help you lose your form, overcome the insistence of the system to appear to you as the ultimate reality. They are designed to help you remember that you are the dreamer, and that, as a dreamer, you are always creating an avatar. Go beyond the limits imposed by the simulation. Go beyond the ways in which the brain is glossing over the stimuli to bring you to a more familiar world, a more predictable world. Go beyond. Discover and experiment. **Dream this dream fearlessly, without prejudice, without fear, without attachment to your form.**

On Lucidity and Apperception

Fear is the first great obstacle. **To overcome fear, nothing like the clarity that comes from knowing that you are dreaming.** This is called lucidity. It is the clarity of mind that comes from realizing this basic fact: that any experience is a dream. However, to simply repeat this like a parrot is not the same as lucidity. It is necessary, not only to say it, not only to believe it but, actually, to realize this truth and see it in its pure clarity.

The following exercise will help you develop lucidity effectively. The trick is to remember yourself and develop a quality of attention that tends to make you aware that you are dreaming.

ᏣᏌᏐᏣᏌᏐ

Whenever you remember, pause and ask yourself: "Is this a dream?" Ask this question often, under any circumstances; and ask it in all seriousness, really trying to find out if this is a dream. Do not just ask the question mechanically to subsequently dismiss it with a shrug of the shoulders, as if you already know you are not. Ask the question and seek evidence that this is a dream. In other words, do not seek for evidence that this is not a dream, but evidence that it is. Test, for example, the solidity of a wall, the temperature of an ice cube. See if you can fly. Look at a book and see if you can read a paragraph without it shifting. Try to speak a language you don't know. See if you can make a unicorn appear. Teleport yourself. Do this often, always asking the question and doing a test.

ᏣᏌᏐᏣᏌᏐ

Many times, you will keep on dreaming, thinking you are awake, and every test you make will "show" you that you are awake … until you wake up and realize that you were dreaming all along. Other times, the dream will reveal itself to you. Either way, something in your awareness is being trained when you ask this question. The cumulative effect of this exercise is the triggering of the ability to become lucid.

CRITIFICATION

Another useful exercise that leads to lucidity is to be performed before going to bed. Have a glass of water next to your bed. Before you retire for the night, clear your head of unnecessary worries and distractions, and your body of remaining tensions. In a state of quiet introspection, hold the glass of water with your fingertips. Feel the energy emanating from your hands, or the pulsations of your fingertips. Gazing into the water, say to yourself: "I will remember my dreams." Then, go to sleep. As soon as you wake up, drink some more of the water, and immediately after drinking the water, start writing in your dream journal.

CRITIFICATION

Using a dream journal is of utmost importance. This recommendation bears repetition. The act of putting dreams to paper brings something from our dreams to the waking, and connects the act of doing in the Tonal (the ordinary world of the known) with the Dreaming through the arm and hand of your organic body. **Write your dreams. Make it a lifelong habit. This is a habit whose rewards you will reap well into your golden years.**

Do not worry about whether you remember your dreams or not. Do not let such an irrelevant issue stop you from writing them in your journal. Every time I am training or working in the Dreaming, I write in my journal as soon as I wake up. I don't worry about what I am going to write, or about whether I remember any dreams or not. I simply take my pen and apply it to the paper. I write whatever flows out of the mind at that moment. I don't criticize it or censor it in any way. I simply write. If you only remember an image, or even just a word, write it down. Begin there. You will notice that, many times, a word is all it takes for the rest of the dream to unravel. And when nothing is there, write that. Just write that you don't remember anything at all, and continue with whatever comes to your mind at that point. As you write, more will come up. This is training your mind to remember the dreams, and the more you train your mind to remember your dreams, the more likely you will be to trigger the awareness that you are dreaming when you are in the middle of a dream. Memory increases awareness, and awareness begets lucidity.

There is only one more term to become familiar with before we can delve deeper into the mysteries and joys of dreaming. When you read these words, it is important to be present. What does this mean? It means that you must make the inner effort to not just have your eyes see the words on the page and your mind parrot the sounds of the words read. You must also be here! You need to be present as you read and as you do the experiments and exercises. An experience is not fully realized unless you can observe it, but it is not fully observed if your attention is somewhere else. There are times when we are going through something, giving the appearance of being fully conscious and awake, but we are somewhat "gone." Have you ever driven all the way home without realizing, or even remembering, all the turns you took to get there? You were there, awake and observing the road, the trees, the cars, and the controls on your panel. Yet, you were not present. The concept we are about to name is the key to attain presence, and therefore the key to master one's perception. This key will enable you not only to become lucid, but to access your true powers as you experience life in the Dreaming, in the waking, and throughout your voyages in the vast immensity of the empyrean—the totality of all dimensions of existence.

This key is called *apperception*. Imagine a flower in front of you. Its petals are of a clear golden hue. Imagine this flower in every detail. See the veins in its petals. Feel the firm yet yielding roundness of its stalk. Touch the soft petals, and the granularity of its center. Observe the shades and nuances of its edges. Now, observe yourself observing this image.

CRES

Let us try something else. Keep reading these words. Slow down the speed of your reading. Observe each word as you keep reading. Now, at this very moment, notice yourself reading this. Observe yourself reading these words. This, right now, the moment when you remember yourself as you observe any experience whatever, is when you use the faculty of apperception.

CRES

Practice the faculty of apperception any time, any moment. Do it as often as you can, for as long as you can. It is a non-phenomenal muscle that needs to be trained. **The faculty of apperception is one of the most powerful techniques you can learn from any esoteric school.** This exercise alone is worth the price of this book. But since you already paid for it, why not read the rest?

With the habit of keeping a dream journal and of exercising the faculty of apperception, you will develop lucidity. Pretty soon, you will be waking up in your dreams and have more and more conscious control of your experiences. Until, one day, you will find yourself awakening during your daily waking life. At that moment, you will fully realize that every experience whatsoever is a dream, and you might even come to know yourself as the dreamer who is having all these experiences in the Palace of Dreams, and experience the true awakening as the One Who Sleeps begins to gain consciousness of yourself as a dreamer.

The Four Regions of the Dreaming

We spend most of our lives in the Dreaming.

In the first place, roughly one third of our day is used in sleep. This time of slumber is used by the body to regenerate damaged tissue, to grow and build material for our organs, and to store and classify the events of our waking life. Sleep is the moment when the body does most of its repairs and adjustments. It is also the time when babies grow the most because this is when the body builds new cells to make organs grow. However, repair and growth of the body is not the only thing that happens when we sleep. We also dream, and a good portion of the dream time is used to classify and store the events of the day.

Our dreaming and the work that we do in the Dreaming constitute a good third of our entire life and our entire work experience. Most of the work that we engage in our conscious, everyday life is only a small percentage of the entirety of the life of our subconscious. The subconscious, being ruled by the tail-brain or the cerebellum, is connected to the autonomic nervous system. Our dreams, just like our subconscious life, are ruled by this central nervous system. To achieve the totality of one's being, the individuation of consciousness, we do need to bring all aspects of ourselves to work for the Work.

When we say "subconscious" or "unconscious," we must understand that we only call it that from the point of view of the ordinary, everyday waking consciousness, but the subconscious mind is awake and conscious in its own right. The dream work, therefore, is a matter of becoming aware of every part of ourselves—that is, of ourselves as divided into two different entities. One of them is the conscious part of us who lives, works and has searched for a spiritual life. It is the conscious *you*. The Dream Self is awake while dreaming. Each one of these two avatars lives in its own environment. One can have a glimpse of the life of the other. We see the life of the Dream Self when we sleep. The Dream Self glimpses our lives when we are awake. In essence, the Waking Self dreams the life of the Dream Self, and the Dream Self dreams our waking life. To become fully aware of our dream life, we need to learn to wake up in the waking and in the dreaming. In this way, the one who dreams both avatars will learn to exercise his or her will in the totality of the experience.

There are four main aspects of dreaming: two involuntary and two voluntary. The involuntary ones are divided into the ordinary dreams and the dreams of the higher self. The voluntary dreams are divided into the work of the etheric double and the work of the astral self.

Let's have a quick look at each of these aspects.

The ordinary, everyday dreams happen at the onset of the REM sleep. They are a mechanism designed for the body to resolve, catalogue and store information received throughout the day. Without this feature, we would go crazy very quickly. It is, in essence, a reboot or reset of our software. When the consciousness is reaching certain levels of awakening, dreams of this type diminish because the consciousness is learning to create this process while awake and conscious. Through meditation and the increase of awareness, one enters into the Dreaming, though not through the REM sleep—which is random, chaotic and, in a certain way, disturbing to the quietude of consciousness. In a way, a dream is a disturbance of sleep just as much as thought is a disturbance of consciousness. With the awakening of higher consciousness, therefore, we begin to enter the Dreaming, not through what we call ordinary dreams, but through the *Sleep of Siloam*.

There is a story associated with this. In the New Testament, Jesus came to a well and he was thirsty. There was a woman by the well and Jesus asked for water. The woman was surprised because she was a Samaritan and to most Jews the Samaritans were less than dogs at that time. She was surprised because he was talking to her. "I ask for a drink of the water from this well. I can give you to drink from a different well," he said to her. "When one drinks of the waters of the well of Siloam, one never thirsts again." **The "waters of Siloam" is an esoteric reference to a place of access to the Dreaming. It is a space outside the Dreaming. It seems as if the consciousness is immersed in a pool of pure, boundless light. A few minutes of exposure to these waters refreshes the mind, the body and the spirit, and it is the entrance to the higher regions of the Dreaming.**

The higher dreaming is comprised of the dreams coming from the higher self. They are also known as *dreams of power*. These are the *initiatory dream*, the *dream triumphant*, and the *nightmare*.

The initiatory dream is an experience that emanates from your higher self and, as the name suggests, prepares your soul for the next step on its path of evolution.

The remaining aspects of the higher dreaming are the dream triumphant and the nightmare. Consider this: before you took this incarnation, you were a being eternal, pure and divine. When you take on this incarnation, that does not change. You are still that being regardless of the actions of your life, regardless of your choices, regardless of your karma. But you took on this lifetime to have an experience and to do a work. Part of your work has to do with awakening your deepest nature through the use of this avatar. But the avatar has its own will, its own wants and desires. At some point, all the will and desires of the avatar become fulfilled by surrendering completely to the will of the being. Before that can happen, however, there is going to be an ongoing struggle between the will of the avatar and the will of the being. **When the avatar is getting closer to the will of the being, your dreams reflect this harmony.** Your dreaming becomes infused with triumphant dreams: dreams of complete fulfillment, dreams of utter joy and happiness. When your actions have been following the will of the avatar and have taken you off course, when they have separated you from the path of your true self, your true self tries its best to bring you back. One of the methods it uses is the nightmare dream. **The nightmare is an attempt by the deep subconscious to let you know that something is wrong.** In this way, the involuntary dream that comes from the higher being is a gauge to help us maintain the course we elected for this lifetime. This is how the involuntary dreaming can be used for our spiritual work.

Now, let us look at the voluntary dreaming. Those are classified into two: the etheric double and the astral double. There are very effective methods for building an etheric body that would allow us to travel anywhere on this planet. This is the lower type of astral travel. This etheric double is constructed with the energy generated by our endocrine system.

The astral body, on the other hand, can take us higher than this plane. In this book I will give you the methods for building and strengthening these bodies. The formation of these bodies is very effective in optimizing the health and the powers of your avatars. You can use them to communicate with anyone and gather information from anywhere. It implies the awakening of your dream self.

Waking Dreaming

It is very important to understand that we are always dreaming. The dreaming never stops. It keeps going in the background, even as we are awake, going about our daily business. When we are sleeping, the senses of our body continue to function just as before: the eyes continue to perceive light, the ears continue to perceive sounds, and the skin continues to register vibrations. The muscles continue to move. The only thing that changes is where our attention is.

When we are awake, our attention is in the external world. Our attention is on that which our senses are perceiving. But when we are sleeping, our attention withdraws into that other environment, the environment where there are dreams. The attention that is placed in this other world was called by the Toltecs the *second attention*. We have access to both attentions—the ordinary, everyday attention and the second attention—at any time, any moment, at will. Most of the time, it is something that happens automatically—a switch. But we can train the consciousness. **We can train the attention to be placed voluntarily, either in the external world or in the Dreaming.**

When we fall asleep, the brain releases a hormone that disconnects our attention from the external senses. It also disconnects our voluntary movements from the musculoskeletal system of the body. This explains why in the Dreaming you can run, you can fight, you can jump, you can say things and none of these actions are transferred to the physical body. They are only happening in the Dreaming. Now, this disconnection that naturally happens when we fall asleep facilitates our attention being placed in the Dreaming. It makes it possible for our attention to withdraw from the outside world, and withdrawing from the outside world leaves all the energy of our consciousness to be placed in the other world—in the Dreaming. For the most part, we run our attention on limited energy. **To be able to access both worlds at the same time is a matter of personal power.**

When we are awake, the external objects have such a pull on our external senses—sight, smell, touch, hearing, sensing—that the attention naturally follows the course of external events. When these sources of attention are disconnected, our attention naturally goes to the Dreaming. With a little bit of training, you can switch easily between one and the other. However, to be able to have access to both at the same time requires also enough energy—energy that we call personal power.

So, we are going to do a simple experiment right now to demonstrate to you, without a doubt, that you are able to perceive both worlds, that you can switch from one to the other, and that you have indeed the capacity to perceive the Dreaming and the waking at will.

C**08**5DCR8D

This is the experiment. Sit in a comfortable posture. Take a slow and deep breath. As you are reading these words, become aware of the periphery of your vision. Now, as your eyes are still centered on this page, move your attention slowly around you and to the back of your head, just as if the attention is a thin membrane that is covering your face, your body, and it's moving around and behind you. And as this membrane passes through your face, you notice on the back of your head you are beginning to become aware of a different space. You don't have to define it. You don't have to analyze it. All you have to do at this moment is to note that it is there. Center and maintain your attention on the back of your head. Allow the impressions to flow through you. They are about to become louder and more defined. There! That is the second attention.

Now move your attention back to where it was before.

ೞೞೞೞ

When you are placing your attention on the back of your head, it is as if you're looking behind you, in front of you, or even on both sides. What you're perceiving at that moment, is only the entrance to the other side. Once you enter that world, the world becomes three-dimensional, and you can see in front or turn around and look behind. And with some experience, you can train yourself to see in a three hundred and sixty degree angle.

The physical sensations you perceive in the back of the head, are psychic impressions, or impressions that come from the second attention. There is an exercise designed to demonstrate the difference between the physical sensations coming through the senses and the psychic sensations coming through the second attention.

ೞೞೞೞ

Place your attention on the front of your forehead—your third eye. Concentrate your attention there like a laser point. Now, move this point through to the back of your head, and continue going just a few inches behind your head. Now, allow that attention to expand behind you. Perceive this membrane of attention expanding behind you. Now, close your physical eyes and look with your second attention above and behind you. Perhaps you will notice that even the words on this page seem to be coming from somewhere else.

In the second attention, notice where the source of light is. Look around the room. After a little exploration, find your organic body. Notice that you have grown bigger than your physical body. Enter your body. Take the shape of your physical body. Take the form of your body. Take a deep breath and fully see with your physical eyes.

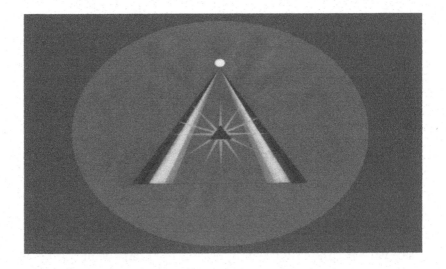

Graphic representation of the Dreaming's Gate full-color card for exercises in this chapter. For the full color, activated art work card, order from this website: https://www.koyotetheblind.com

Dreaming's Gate

The trick to having access to other planes of existence is to realize that we exist in different places simultaneously.

When you are playing a video game, your consciousness is both, in the room where your physical body is and in the avatar that is moving and experiencing the game environment, at the same time. When you immerse yourself in the story line, your consciousness identifies with the actions and experiences of the avatar, and you feel like what is happening to it is also happening to you. You might even forget your physical surroundings at moments. You suffer, fear, and enjoy as the avatar does. When you have to adjust your back, have some food, or answer a question in the room where your physical body exists, you pull your consciousness and your identity away from the gaming avatar and into your physical form.

The same principle is active whenever you dream.

When you dream, you create a dream avatar. This dream avatar is designed to move in and experience the environment created in the Dreaming. You create a dreaming self through which you experience the dream. Are you not also in your physical body? Of course you are. You are in both your organic body and in your dream body simultaneously.

How much you perceive the dream as "real" depends on the level of abstraction and identification you attain in that dream. As your consciousness abstracts from the stimuli of the physical senses, your attention naturally fixates itself on the stimuli coming from the Dreaming. Similarly, when you wake up and the attention moves from the Dreaming to the physical world around you, the Dreaming fades to the background and places itself on the signals coming through the physical senses.

We must understand, however, that we are always dreaming.

When we are awake and our attention is centered in the physical world around us, the subconscious continues to dream. There are inner dialogs going on inside us: images of past events, judgments about what is going on right now, questions popping up, and even full-on dreams unfolding in the subconscious. **Yes, the dream world does not stop just because we wake up. The dream continues; we just withdraw our attention from it and place it fully on the waking.** If during our waking life we happen to withdraw our attention from the stimuli of the physical senses, we experience day dreams and, at times, even full-on dreams when we are not sleeping. When we fall asleep, we withdraw our attention from the physical senses almost completely and, therefore, we enter fully into the action of the dream world.

The same thing can be said when we are dreaming. It is not that the waking world is not there. The physical world is still there, we just have withdrawn our attention from it. Notice that, even though we close our eyes when we sleep, our five senses continue to operate. The skin registers temperature and movement, just like when it's awake. The ear drums continue to receive sound vibrations. The nose continues to receive and register smells. In fact, even the eyes continue to receive light through closed eyelids. Yet, even though the senses still operate, we do not seem to be aware of the stimuli. This is because we do not really stop receiving it, but simply withdraw our attention from it.

The following is the key to learning to consciously go from the waking to the dreaming and, indeed, to any other plane of existence where we have formed a body:

You must learn to withdraw your attention from one plane and place it on another at will.

If your attention is placed on the external world, on the stimulation coming from your physical senses, then you will withdraw your attention from the inner world of the Dreaming. But, if you know that the Dreaming is always there, it is a matter of just moving your attention from the world your senses perceive and placing it on the inner world.

This movement might seem hard to do at first, but it is actually very, very simple and easy. It is so easy that we do it every day and every night. The difficulty is not in withdrawing the attention from one plane and placing it on another, since we do that every day. The difficulty is learning to do it at will. It is a movement, a switch, we have been doing automatically, like breathing and the beating of our heart; but just like breathing, we can also decide to do it voluntarily.

You can choose where your attention will be placed.

You can use the Dreaming's Gate to train yourself to gain mastery of your attention, to access your dream world at will; and later, even, to use this ability to access higher planes of consciousness.

This tool will train different parts of your psyche, your attention, and your dream self. The first part of the training consists of training the attention to switch from the outer to the inner and to keep it where you want it to stay. Here is the first exercise:

1. Find a place where you can be alone and undisturbed for about five minutes.
2. Minimize external distractions of sound, smell, and light. You need enough light to see the Dreaming's Gate, but don't have your television on or anything else that will be shining on your eyelids.
3. Sit in a comfortable position you can hold for five minutes without discomfort.
4. Stare at the Dreaming's Gate for 30 to 45 seconds without blinking and without moving your eyes. Stare with as much attention and intensity as you can muster.
5. Close your eyes.
6. Place your attention on the inner image that appears in your mind's eye, and hold it for as long as you can. At first, the image might vanish after a few seconds, change, or distort itself in some way.
7. Repeat steps 4 to 6 as many times as you like, but stop if you are getting tired or sleepy.
8. Keep working with this exercise until you are able to hold the image without change for at least one minute.

C3ED CR80

This exercise will allow you to place and hold your attention in the inner spaces at will and strengthen your attention to be able to withdraw from the senses, also at will. Mastering this exercise will make it possible for you to master all the exercises given in *The Golden Flower.*

In fact, this exercise and the next two will prove to be an effective way to train your psychic attention to be able to travel in the Dreaming, to gain the ability to become lucid in your dreams, and also to awaken many latent psychic abilities you didn't know you had.

After you have gained the ability to hold the after-image of the Dreaming's Gate for a minute or more, it is time to train your mind to access the gate any time, at will.

CRSOCRSO

1. Find a comfortable and safe place where you can be undisturbed.
2. Sit or lie down comfortably.
3. Close your eyes and see the Dreaming's Gate in your mind's eye.
4. Visualize it with as much detail as possible: colors, shapes, and all other details.
5. Compare it with the physical copy until you can visualize it without distortion.

CRSOCRSO

For this exercise, it is okay if, instead of using a phantom image, as you did in the previous exercise, you imagine it. Imagination is good for this exercise. **Later, you'll realize that the imagination is a powerful gateway to the Dreaming and, indeed, to any other plane of existence.**

The third and final exercise with the Dreaming's Gate will suggest itself to you. It might happen after you have mastered the first two, or it can happen as you are still working with them. This exercise will open the gates to the Dreaming and allow you to enter it, and the astral plane, consciously and at will.

CᴚᏕᎧᏟᏕᎧ

1. Hold the Dreaming's Gate in your mind's eye without distortions.
2. As soon as you feel a pull or the sensation of movement, go through the triangle.
3. You can travel anywhere you desire, and you will have many adventures. If at any point you want to come back, simply will yourself to come back to the body. Or, you can bring the Dreaming's Gate to your mind's eye and walk backwards away from it and into your physical body.
4. When you come back, take a few seconds to feel the body and feel yourself re-entering your body.
5. Record your experience in detail. It is very important to write every experience down.

CᴚᏕᎧᏟᏕᎧ

Enjoy your travels and experiences with this powerful and ancient tool! It was provided by my benefactor, and it has been used by countless shamans, Toltec initiates, and magicians. It is charged with their intent, and it is an extraordinary tool for voyaging and mastering the inner worlds.

The Key of Dreams

We were saying before that the dream world can be divided into its conscious and unconscious aspects. In the most unconscious and automatic parts of dreaming, we have the type of dreaming we get when we first fall asleep and enter into that REM state of sleep. This type of dreaming is pretty much a recollection and cataloging of loose impressions collected throughout the day. Those dreams are not really that significant. They are mostly loose impressions, remnants of the waking life. The body and the consciousness have to somehow recover those pieces of data that we leave behind while not paying attention to what we're doing, carelessly going through the mechanical events of our daily life. These are the dreams that happen during the first part of the night, the first couple of hours.

Now, while the images that we're cataloging are not significant when we are working on ourselves, there is going to be a definite shift in the quality of our work which will be signaled by a change in these early dreams. The shift that I'm speaking of has to do with being able to enter the Dreaming without the REM sleep. Remember that this REM dreaming[1] happens because of all the uncatalogued, loose

---

1 While the literature refers always to "REM sleep" and never to "REM dreams," I use the latter here because it is a far more accurate moniker, not only because we are ostensibly dealing with the Dreaming itself without covering the physical neural correlates, but also because the REM sleep itself is, according to some, a misnomer. REM sleep has been called "paradoxical sleep," because the brain behaves as if it was awake. Most of the neural firing and hormonal activity operates during REM sleep as if we were awake, but we are dreaming and transitioning into full physiological sleep. With extensive work on dreaming, I've come to realize that the type of dreaming activity that occurs during REM sleep occurs at times when awake, while doing other activities; and with training, we can voluntarily trigger these dreams at will and open a doorway to experience other planes of existence or lucid dreams.

impressions that we have not been paying attention to throughout the day. With work on self, with the growing of our consciousness, we learn to live life more and more as a meditation, as an awakening. When that happens, we enter into the Dreaming having very little interference from the mind, and we enter into a sleep without the disturbance of dreams.

In the pure light of consciousness, dreams come as a disturbance of this pure light. When we are awake, this disturbance comes in the form of mind-stuff and thoughts. When we sleep, this disturbance comes in the form of dreams. **Therefore, as your increase in awareness and personal power becomes more evident, you will have a definite marker of your purpose when you enter your dreaming, as if you found yourself immersed in a field of pure light, unperturbed by dreams.**

After a few hours of sleep and a few hours before you wake up, that's when you can have the type of dreaming that is of tremendous significance for your spiritual life. The Great Work can, in part, be described as making the unconscious conscious. The unconscious is truly a very conscious and knowledgeable aspect of Self. The unconscious contains the accumulated experience and knowledge of humanity. This unconscious, which is both personal and collective, is what evolves through the performance of the Great Work. It has been guiding us from the moment we were born until the moment we die. Since the moment of birth, it knows what we came here to do, what we came here to accomplish, and what we came here to experience. At the moment of death, on the other hand, it collects all the experiences of life and registers it in the astral light that surrounds the biosphere of the planet. These impressions in the astral light, containing all activity on the planet, has been called the *Akashic records.*

Part of the guidance of this older and higher intelligence is through the subtle communication with our ego, a communication that happens through dreams, through intuition and through synchronicity encountered in everyday life. **The type of communication that happens in the dreams of power are seen as a direct communication from the eternal divine mind inside yourself with your ego.** It communicates with the ancient language of symbols. It communicates through those symbols that have been acquired through the aeons by humanity.

There are three types of dreams of power. The first one is the dream triumphant. The dream triumphant refers to those dreams that make a clear impression in your soul, giving you deep satisfaction, tremendous pleasure, joy, knowledge, and the unmistakable sensation that you have just done something really good. This type of dreaming is a good signal that you are in alignment with your destiny, your dharma, your path of life, your will. It signals that you are creating a life that is in agreement with the cosmic, divine purpose of your incarnation. In other words, it's the type of dream that tells you that you are going in a good direction.

The second type of significant dream is the initiatory dream. The initiatory dream is a dream that contains sacred archetypes. The older the archetypes, the more powerful the dream. In this dream, you go through something like death, rebirth, and initiation. You might encounter creatures like serpents, stars, grandfathers or any number of archetypes. In some of these dreams you go through a definite initiatory process. This type of initiatory dream tells you that you are now working at a new level. It gives you a knowledge and a level of energy that you did not have before. It marks a new beginning.

There is a third type of dream of power that usually happens right before you wake up, and this is what we call the nightmare dream. Just as the dream triumphant tells you that you are in alignment with your pure will, the nightmare dream signals the opposite: it is a desperate attempt from your pure will, from the divine guidance inside yourself, to tell you that you are betraying something crucial and fundamental. It signals to you with that direct discomfort in your soul that you need to get back on course.

When you learn to see your higher dreaming from the perspective of a channel of communication from the deepest level of your subconscious with your ego, you will enter a radically different relationship with your dreaming.

People often ask me questions about children having nightmares. Most of these nightmares involve archetypes such as vampires, witches, clowns, etc. The archetypes signal that the dream is a dream of power. A key question here is whether the child is perturbed during the dream or if the child is made to be afraid after the dream. If it's the first scenario, then that dream is a dream that is trying to guide the child. It's trying to give impressions to the child so that the child instinctively and automatically seeks the experiences that he or she needs for this lifetime. If the fear comes after the child tells the dream, then that is simply the unconscious and automatic influence that the adults are trying to have on that child. In any case, the dream is the guidance that the child is receiving from her own unconscious. Those are dreams that need to happen and will happen. They will guide the child by providing her with the correct archetypal language that she will need throughout her life.

If you understand this point, you will become a master of your dreams. **The point is this: you and me, all of us, are under guidance. There is something eternal, divine and of vastly superior intelligence guiding us—guiding you individually and guiding us collectively through an evolutionary process.** The language that this being is using is refining itself the more we understand this language. All the sacred books that humanity has produced, all the teachers who have tirelessly worked to teach us, all the great works of art, conscious art, all the tales and fables, even the history of humanity, with all its horrors and all its glories, are helping refine the language we use to communicate with this higher intelligence. The oneiric language is part of the most intimate and most ancient of languages that we use to communicate.

It is important, when these communications from the Dreaming happen, that your actions begin to match the message. In other words, this higher intelligence is guiding you and is telling you, "Here, come back to your center." Or it's telling you, "Yes, keep going in that direction." Whether because you understood the concept consciously, or simply because your intuition is being guided by the feelings evoked by these unremembered dreams, the important thing is that your actions begin to match the intended result of the dream. In the process of learning, we want to become more and more conscious of this message.

Both the dream triumphant and the nightmare are dreams of power. The nightmare is a dream of power. It is simply a dream that is telling you that something is off, that something needs to be corrected, that something that is being betrayed needs to be put right.

Endeavor in all things to see all experiences from the same point of view. Whether in the Dreaming, whether in ordinary life, whether in your sacred temple, know that all and every experience is a dealing of God with your soul. Then, for every event in life and for every dream, you will ask yourself, "What is the intended message?" This will give you the key to understanding all dreams and all experiences.

In short, you must endeavor to increase your consciousness by knowing that, in every moment, whether asleep or awake, you are dialoguing with your heart; you are encountering God. No matter what seems to be happening, no matter how pleasant or unpleasant, this moment is a dealing between divine creatures. To know this will result in the evolution of your consciousness.

The Seven Bodies of Man
E. J. Gold

Part Two

And the Flower Unfolds
Petals of Light

Across the Borders of the Dreaming

I discovered the tenuous membrane that separates the Dreaming from the waking one bright morning in the suburbs of San Salvador. I had been looking forward to the start of kindergarten. My mother was a teacher in a public school. She worked in the afternoon, which allowed me to spend the occasional afternoon in her classroom. At times, I would accompany her, and once I started learning the alphabet and reading simple sentences, I would sit in her classroom to work on writing my letters and to read children's stories. One day, she told me she had a student that could sell her a little Matchbox toy car and asked me if I wanted one. I got very excited because I had dreamt about that car. I told her that it had to be the kind with doors you can open and see the details inside. The car, however, was taking longer to manifest than my impatience allowed. It could be that I had been waiting for only a few days, but in my eagerness, I could have sworn it was weeks.

So, I kept asking, "Did you get the car?"

Each time she would give the same patient answer, "No, not yet. Pedro is still looking for it."

Instead of feeling disappointed about not getting the car, I would get more excited imagining it. One Saturday morning, before waking up to watch the two hours of cartoons on Channel 4, I stayed in bed a little longer than usual. I was having a very good dream with my car. It was a '65 Chevy convertible, I came to learn many years later. I was holding it in my hands, opening its doors and even the trunk. As I began to wake up, I realized the dream was about to dissolve before the light of day inundated my awareness. There, in that liminal state

41

between dreaming and waking, I tried to hold on to my toy car. I could feel it in my right hand. I felt its solid frame and cold material. Being aware that I was waking up made it really hard to hold on to the dream, but as the dream itself dissolved into the darkness of my consciousness, I managed to hold on to the sensation of the toy car. I held on to the feeling in my hand. I kept my hand closed, feeling the sensation of the car as my mind slowly woke up and the sound and light of the morning became prominent. I started to hear the birds outside, smell the aroma of my father's cup of coffee, and feel the bedsheets and pajamas on my skin. But out of sheer desire, I managed to also retain the sensation of the car I had played with in my dream. It was there, in my hand. Once the consciousness of daytime had fully asserted itself, and I could still feel the car inside my fist, I began to consider a thought that would appear many times over in my childhood and adolescence, a whisper that would ask me over and over again: "What if magick is real?"

On that morning of 1969, I almost felt sure it was, as I realized that I was fully awake and could still feel the car in my hand. I wondered if I could have possibly managed to bring something from my dream into the physical world. Something in me thought that was possible, and this promising thought would emerge many times in so many different ways in my life. Could it be true that miracles happen? Was magick real—a reality as fantastic and amazing as it appears in my dreams and in the stories people tell? And what about beyond that? Could it be that there are worlds and things of wonder and fulfilling happiness? Could there really be a world where I can play and explore and no one tries to kill, imprison, torture? Can I laugh and love and not worry about people making others hungry and sick in a world without murder and pain? These questions would come up repeatedly in formulations in accordance to my level of development.

42

That day, however, I felt I had almost answered my question in the affirmative, as I became convinced that I would open my hand and my car would still be there, and would remain with me after the dream had long become vanished and forgot. I could still feel a seed of doubt in my mind, however, and somehow I knew already that this doubt would block the ability to make something extraordinary happen. Did I know this from a previous life? From being in tune with the over-mind, humanity's collective unconscious? From somehow being aware of the entire lifetime I was beginning to live once again? From having a budding connection with the source of knowledge? From mere inspiration and the imagination of an emerging story teller? I don't really know from where this idea came, but I know that, that morning, I struggled against a doubt under my consciousness by attempting to master my sensation:

If I can hold on to the sensation of the toy car in my hand as I wake up and keep feeling it past the point of regaining full waking consciousness, then perhaps I will also bypass the doubts and make it happen.

Finally, when I could be sure that the sensation in my hand was there, that I had mastered the ability to feel it even in full waking consciousness, I opened my hand with the clear expectation that I was about to witness something awesome. When I saw my empty hand, I began to feel the sensation of the car dissolving back into the dreaming, merging behind the loud clarity of the morning. I went about my day, going to Los Siete Enanitos kindergarten— with its fairytale, child-sized statues in the patio—and Ivan, a little kid clutching at the entrance gate, crying for his mom. I became acquainted with the smell of playdough and the trick of failing to color within the borders. In the afternoon, after forgetting most of what happened that day and the dream incident no longer at the forefront of my mind, my mom came home from work with a surprise for me. It was the exact same model of toy car I had dreamt with! I held it in my hands, and I felt it, just like I did in that liminal state I found myself in between dreaming and waking, as I tried to hold on to the perceptions and sensations of the desired toy.

It seemed to me like I had stumbled upon a secret way to bring a dream into my waking life. A few years later, I had another occasion to put that into practice. I was in the fourth grade in an all-boys Jesuit school in San Salvador. I didn't have money for the bus, and I could not call anyone to come pick me up. Usually, I would just walk home. The walk home took almost one hour. On this day, however, I had to get home on time because it was Thursday, the day I went with my friend Ivan, the now grown little boy crying and holding onto the gates to the *Siete Enanitos*, and his family, to listen to the classical music orchestra downtown. I was walking the hallways of the third floor of the school building. The building was designed as a four stairs quad, in the middle of which there was a walkway in the form of a cross dividing four square patches of grass. The elementary grades were on the bottom floor. The middle grades were on the second floor, and the high school grades on the third floor. The fourth floor was designed to be the living quarters of the Jesuit priests.

I liked roaming after hours—roaming everywhere, especially where I didn't belong. I liked visiting a small chapel on the third floor where, one day, my friend Quiroz and I saw the statue of a crucified Jesus open its mouth. We ran before we could hear what he wanted. I would come to this chapel to pray and to be alone with my thoughts. This day, it had gotten late, and I was turning one of the corners of the third floor corridor, when I realized I had spent all my money and had none to get back home. I started to panic because my parents were no longer living in the city and the aunt I was living with had no car. When I came to the top of the stairs that lead down to the school's office and reception area, I paused and closed my eyes. I found inside me the space I had been in when praying in the chapel. The cobwebs of thoughts of worry and impossibilities were removed; and I saw there, in my mind, two coins: a shiny five and the larger ten cents coin. They were in the back of my mind, as if I was dreaming them. Fifteen cents is what I needed for the bus, and there was in me a certainty about this image, and a decision to feel these coins in my hands. I proceeded to descend the stairs, and right after the bend that would lead me to the first floor, right on one of the steps, I saw the shinning nickel and the bigger ten cent Salvadoran coin. At this point, I said to myself:

Remember this.
You can always find what you can see.

The Yoga of Dreaming

Let us start with the understanding that, in truth, we're always dreaming. That which we call *dreaming* is always happening. The activity of images, sounds, stories, routines and sub-routines are always going on in the subconscious. When we are awake, that stream of consciousness that we call *dreaming* is active, albeit muted. When awake, our attention is fixated on the input that comes through the senses and on the stream of consciousness that passes through our conscious mind. There, in the external senses and the thinking mind, is where we place our attention; and for most of us, that also includes the emotional manifestations of the ordinary emotional centrum.

The noise coming through the senses is so loud and overwhelming, when we are awake, that we barely perceive the motions and the events of the dream. Then, when we go to bed and we begin to fall asleep, our attention disconnects from the input coming from the body and the input coming from the thinking centrum; and the attention goes through a reset period, a brief reset period as the brain and nervous system begin to catalog the events of the day; taking slices of experiences, sounds and images; and storing them in the muscular system of the body. We perceive, in a fleeting way, a parade of images and events that occurred to us during the day. Later in the night, as the body has been going through its process of healing, rejuvenation and recuperation, we enter into the realm of the Dreaming.

We have already covered the four kinds of dreaming that we can speak of. The first one is what happens as we drift into sleep, and it is the dreaming which is a mechanical cataloging of the events of the day. Then, there is the healing dreams which can come in two forms. They can either be nightmare dreams, where something essential in us finds itself slightly deviated from its path; and the nightmare is an attempt by the subconscious to right a wrong, to bring back into balance something that has shifted too much towards an unbalanced state.

The nightmare dream is not a bad dream. It is a corrective dream. Its counterpart, the other side of the coin, is the triumphant dream. This is a dream where archetypal images in the mind are completing a process. The archetypes are completing an event in our subconscious that allows more and more of our hidden presence to become manifest to us.

The triumphant dream is a dream that comes when we are in balance and in harmony with our pure will— the reason for our incarnation. In both cases, these dreams are an attempt by our system to align itself to its master. The body is a carriage, it is a vehicle that carries our presence and consciousness. As a vehicle, it is designed to be the avatar of the essence—an avatar that can carry the consciousness of the essence throughout this incarnation, to experience and to perform its work. **The dreams are cataloging our experiences into the subconscious, but at the same time, they are consciously adjusting this finely tuned instrument, our consciousness, to the will and the attention of the essential self.**

During our waking life, this continues to happen, but we are oblivious to it. We don't see it because our ordinary attention is placed on the external world and in the chatter of our mind. Sometimes our higher self, the essential being who is eternal and always part of the Body of God, speaks to us. It is telling us the key to progress in our work, telling us the stories of our divine origin, guiding us, giving us more light and more understanding. Sometimes, it speaks through the synchronicities in our daily life. Sometimes, it speaks through our teachers and, sometimes, directly through our intuition and our dreams. When speaking through our dreams and intuition, the voice of that inner silence resonates through that part of ourself that dreams. We receive that voice as a whisper into the heart; and we receive that voice as a sudden insight, a knowing that came to us, not as the result of induction or deduction, but as direct gnosis, a knowing.

There are times we engage the spiritual path from our conscious mind, but the conscious mind is so small a pond in comparison to the ocean that is the subconscious. We engage the Great Work with the best of intentions, and we're trying to go one way while our subconscious is going a different way. **The key to attainment is to unify these two states of consciousness, waking and dreaming, and have them both be ruled by a higher authority— the authority of the essential self.** This essential self finds itself inhabiting an avatar—an avatar that exists with a physical body and a human identity in the waking world and, at times, finds itself inside an avatar in the dream world, made of the very dream-stuff dreams are made of.

The source of the attention that executes all its work in the waking is also working in the Dreaming. We don't always know it. We don't always remember it, but a teacher who has unified his consciousness will be guiding, teaching, providing shocks and opportunities in both realms. When you move from one side to the other, the side you're paying attention to acquires detail, vibrancy and color, and your attention becomes so immersed in what you are witnessing that the other side fades away into the background and you do not fully remember. In the waking, the dreams become disconnected flashes of memory slowly fading away from your consciousness as your attention becomes rooted in the input of the senses. Then, when you find yourself in a dream, your waking life fades also into the background, becoming forgotten and barely accessible from where you are.

And so, we go from one dream to another, from one experience to another, never fully remembering ourselves, never connecting the threads of events that form the totality of our consciousness.

The unification of our experiences—the experiences of the waking and the experiences of the dream—is an essential component to the aim of unifying our being so that, as a complete avatar present in this world and all the others, it can listen to the voice of the master, the essence, the divine spark of consciousness within us—because that voice of the essence is not divided. It is unified. It is unique. It is undivided. When it speaks, it is heard differently from the divided consciousness. The mind hears it a certain way, the emotions hear it in a different way, and the subconscious (through the dreaming) hears it yet another way.

All to create a tapestry of consciousness that moves between the Dreaming and the waking as the slithering serpent of fire unifies and weaves all the strands of consciousness, creating a unity between the waking and the Dreaming, between life and death, between this life and all the others, between the self and the non-self, until the whole of experience is one vast field of light and there is no longer a division between the experience of one dream and the experience of another dream—one where consciousness and unconsciousness are equal parts of the ebb and flow of consciousness, the cusp and the crest of this wave— which is consciousness following its serpent path between light

and darkness, finding the essence of being always hovering between darkness and light, such as the Morning Star does— ever present in that liminal state between a sleep and a dream....

To work this serpent path of the Yoga of Dreaming requires an effort of the attention, the effort to remember myself within every dream. It requires the effort to remember that I am dreaming; to know that here, in this room, having this experience in this chamber right now, is a dream; that the dream will resolve itself into nothingness; and that I will be reborn into another dream, and this dream will put itself together from the elements of my mind, and it will resolve itself and, in each resolution of itself, all the opposites merge, combine, recombine and annihilate one another.

When we acquire the experience of remembering that we are in a dream, we will begin to observe this ebb and flow of consciousness, this observing and resolving of the dream back into nothing. We will see, once we have accumulated billions of years of practice, that the currents of experience in the waking and in the Dreaming are following the same laws that create life and destroy life. And so, we will witness, not only dream after dream, experience after experience, but on a larger scale, also life and death and the spaces in between, until we come to see that the entirety of existence is emerging out of the empty void. It combines and recombines itself over and over, always resolving itself back into nothing.

And so, in this union of the I Am within you that observes your lives and observes your dreams, you will find yourself identified with the point of consciousness, eternal and ever present, that has existed from the beginning of creation and will continue to exist until the last flame of the last star fades away; and as such, it has been ever present, existing as you, as me, as everyone

else, having all the dreams, living all the experiences until it too resolves itself back into the nothing whence it came; and in that union of the conscious with the unconscious, in that union between being and not-being, comes the unity of the totality of your being.

Such a grandiose plan, however, starts with a single moment—the moment of today, of right now. And as we speak and hear and see the room we are in, we can become aware that there has been this vast ocean of darkness behind us, moving and sliding in between the words, bringing flashes of images and memories and insights, and every word and every image and every knowing emerges from this tremendous darkness, and goes back to it; and so, everything dissolves itself back into the source of all dreams. **You can observe, as you read these words, that you can become aware that every word emerges out of nothing. Every word is enveloped in nothing and resolves itself into nothing.** Every word, just like every idea, every sentence, and every unit of meaning exists for a brief moment, and the only thing that strings all these words and meanings together is the thread of your consciousness, who lives for a little longer than each word; and thus, it is able to stream a serpent of meaning, creating in that weaving a sense of understanding, a glimpse of memory, a particle of eternal existence.

You can also notice as you read that it is truly a matter of choice where you put your attention. It can be in the dreams that flow across the back of your head, or in the nothingness that sees everything born out of it and everything returned to it, or in the input that comes through the senses and are filtered by the mask of the avatar you have created to have a life to live in a world and to define an identity through the telling of personal stories—the recounting of a dream that you call your life.

That placement of the attention is the one true power we all have and the one true freedom we can all exercise until the time when the avatar has been created out of the totality of one's existence—where a higher sense of being, of freedom, and of personal power can be exercised. And yet, this freedom to place our attention where we will is rarely, very rarely, claimed as one's own. It is here, then, when claiming the power to place your attention, that the true act of creation begins.

CALOGORSO

There is one simple exercise that I have found very useful; take on the habit for one month, every day and every moment, to remember yourself, to look around you and say, "I am dreaming this." And then, if you have time for more than that, examine this dream in all details. Examine the shapes, the colors. Touch! Touch something and marvel at the detail of this hallucination, of this dream. Do that wherever you find yourself, regardless of whether you think that this is a dream or that this is the waking. Learn to see everything as a dream that you're having at this moment. That is one practice to help you remember yourself throughout the dreaming.

The Organic Blueprint of a Soul

There is a part of the brain that is in charge of receiving all the raw data from the senses of the organic body. Everything that is being registered by the skin, by the ear drums, by the eyes, the olfactory and gustatory receptors, is all coming in at once— unadulterated and without discrimination. Every signal that comes into the system is coming to an area at the base of the brain in charge of receiving all the information from the senses and choosing what to let pass to the other parts of the brain. This information comes to the brain first as raw data. It has not yet been catalogued; it has not been put into any kind of order; it has not been filtered yet. It is all there as the organism perceives it. This area at the base of the brain filters the information first. The classification and ordering comes later.

The senses of the physical body are only able to perceive a limited range of vibrations. Even within this limited range, the information would be so overwhelming that, if the brain was not filtering most of the input out, we would be unable to distinguish what we are perceiving. There would be so much noise, so much light, so much perception that it would be impossible to navigate, to make decisions, or to assess the situation around us. The brain, first of all, decides what input is going to be passed on to the appropriate areas of the brain where it is going to be coded, it's going to be put in order, it's going to be stored, and it's going to be analyzed completely by very fast processes. We have created this environment in the brain, this three-dimensional hallucination, which is a holographic representation of the world around us. This thing that we call reality is a holographic representation of what the senses are receiving, and we have to understand that most of what the senses receive ends up being discarded. Most of it doesn't make it. Most of it is set aside as being completely irrelevant, destructive, or distracting. The brain has been constructing this reality from the moment we were born. It has been pruning the input received from the outside world, and from that, we successfully manage to create the world. We know we have successfully created the world when the tribe into which we were born acknowledges us as full members of the tribe and we are able to navigate this world and communicate with the other members that we see this world as they see it.

I find myself inside this simulation of reality, and I encounter other avatars in it. Those avatars are also creations within my simulation that stand for other people: the father, the mother, the friend, the brother, the enemy, the stranger. I assign specific names to each avatar. In order to effectively navigate my way through this environment—which presents itself to me as a very elaborate world full of mysteries, full of dangers and rewards, full of friends and enemies—I have to also create a representation of myself. I must create an avatar, which is an image that carries my own consciousness. I create this avatar inside the simulation. It is my own avatar. It is what I call *myself*. This *myself* is an image designed to live inside my reality construct. I find the other avatars that look at me, interact with me, talk about me and give me feedback. I encounter the ones who are happy, who are sad, who are angry, who attack me, who feel attacked by me, those who are my friends, those who are my family; and I live a life inside this environment; and this life keeps changing.

The environment keeps changing. I keep adding new information. I keep discarding ideas that no longer work, and so it goes. This three-dimensional representation that my brain is creating has been created following learned patterns; patterns of behavior, language, and interactions that I have learned from the other avatars I find inside this simulation. It is obvious, then, that this simulation that I have created over time, by engaging the senses with my frontal cortex, is pretty much a dream in its own right. It is not the reality, as it actually and factually exists outside myself, that I am engaging with. I am engaging it but indirectly. I am engaging it from a control center: this brain, which by itself is not directly perceiving the world outside of me. It is only perceiving the world as it has been recreated inside myself.

Now, the brain is a highly efficient filing system, and as such, it is programmed to leave out most of the information that comes in and to use the data bank that it has created over the years. In fact, for humans, this data bank has been accumulating archetypes, stories, and world views over millennia. Let me give you an example. When you are driving and your eyes are centered on the road in front of you, you see the visual information that comes through. Then, you look at the rear view mirror, and you look at the side mirrors. Then, you look at your speedometer. Then, you look at the road again. Then, you look at the person you are talking to. Then you look, again, at the road. You look at the sign on the side of the road, and so on. Now, when the eyes move from one point to another, the receptors in the eyes can perceive what they are looking at when they are not moving. Then, when the eyes move from point A to point B, they cease to record what is in between point A and point B. They only see point A, and then they see point B; and in between, the eyes are blind. The eyes don't see anything when they are moving. We only see that point where our eyes are focusing. We see point A and we see point B; between point A and point B, darkness. Yet, it doesn't appear to be that way. Even if you try it right now and look at the page in front of you, and then look to the side, at a second point inside the room where you are, it will seem like you see this blurry image that moves through, and then you see point B; and when you come back, you again see a blurry image passing by very quickly, then you come to point A again. Now, that blurry image, we have come to believe and act as if it is something real that we are watching; and yet, what is happening is that the brain is filling in the information, making us believe that we are seeing a world that is real and three-dimensional in front of us. Yet, we know from neuroscience that we do not see it. The brain represents it, and it is the same thing with colors and shadings. Colors are not something that we perceive directly from the world. Rather, our brain fills in the colors on what we see so that we are able to perceive as if we are seeing in three dimensions, as if we are seeing nuances of shape, of size, and of perspective.

Every eye receives a two-dimensional impression. The brain puts together these two images that the eyes receive and present it to the brain as a three-dimensional perspective, so we seem to be watching a three-dimensional world but, in fact, we are looking at a simulation of a three-dimensional world put together from two-dimensional images. Now, the brain does this, not to deceive us. The brain does this because this has been the way in which we are dealing with the natural world around us; and every species of living creatures on the planet is attempting the same thing, attempting to find a way to attune their organism to the optimal way of dealing with the world outside. We have created this human dimension in order to be able to live in this world; but, for the most part, we never perceive the world directly; we only perceive it through the senses. We perceive it within the dream that we have created, based on the input that we are choosing from the senses.

This three-dimensional hallucination we call reality has been formed in the exact same way that a dream is formed, and those dreams are being formed over and over again in a much more fluid manner in the back of our head.

When we shift our attention from the frontal cortex to the back of the head as we fall asleep, we find ourselves in a different environment which we call a *dream*. But, in the moment that we find ourselves in that dream, for the most part, we think that we are experiencing reality; and that reality we experience inside a dream has its own internal logic, its own laws, its own sequence of events, and its own memories; and so, we are able to do and perceive things that seem absurd, illogical, and impossible in the waking world. **The difference between a dream and the waking is not the difference between fantasy and reality, it is rather the difference between different environments that our brain has created.**

The attention can be placed in one environment or the other, just as in this moment you are able to place your attention on the book you are reading, finding yourself in an environment created by the images and ideas presented by the book, resulting in the muting of the information received from the room where your physical body is sitting. In other words, the more attention you place on the details of the book in front of you, the less information you receive from the room where your physical body sits. If something calls your attention in your physical surroundings, your attention will move away from the page and go to the door, to the window, to the child talking to you; and, as you do that, you will notice that a lot of the attention that you were placing on the virtual world is removed so that you can place it in your physical world.

There might be residual attention on one world as you move to the other; but, once you find yourself immersed in the new simulation, in the new world, whether it is another dream or the waking, you begin to loose your hold on that vanishing reality where you used to be just a moment ago. The power of attention is the power to move from one world to the other, from one dream to the other.

When we manage, by will and attention, to retain a memory of where we were just a moment ago, then we can begin to remember our voyages through our dreams, through other worlds, and even through this three-dimensional hallucination we call *life*. This attention can be trained to be moved at will; and so, at will, regardless of whether you are sleeping or awake, you can choose to place it on the information that is being gathered by the frontal cortex, which is to say, on the information that is being gathered through the cerebellum. In other words, you can choose to perceive the consensus reality of the waking or the subconscious reality of the dream. This can be done at any time. This can be done at will, and similarly, if you are in the middle of the dream, you can become aware of what is occurring in that simulation of the waking world that your frontal cortex is creating, so that, within the dream, you become lucid. In other words, within a dream, you remember yourself as the avatar that you have in the waking world.

In the waking world, your dream self can become lucid by remembering itself as the dream self that you create when you dream. Both, together, represent the totality of your being, which is not yet the highest and most true manifestation of yourself. It is only the unification of all the avatars that you have created, whether in the Dreaming or the waking, acquiring a continuity of consciousness that allows you to make decisions under will, regardless of what dream you seem to be going through at the moment.

To do this, to attain to the awareness of the totality of our being, we must become absolutely responsible for our experience and for our perception. We must come to terms with the fact that the reality we perceive, whether it is in a dream or in the waking, is the product of how we are dealing with the infinite light that is bombarding our senses at every moment. We have to come

to terms with the fact that we have created a world divided by time and space inside ourselves, and that we have also created an image of ourselves to be able to navigate this simulation.

If I forget myself, I will come to see this avatar as my true self. This is not my true self; this avatar is passing through a dream in this lifetime. It is attacked. It is offended. It might be killed. Or, it might suffer through illness and injustice. And yet, it is not I who is going through all that. It is I perceiving all that, but through an avatar that only exists inside this dream, that only exists inside this simulation; and I have created countless other avatars in other worlds, in other dreams; and I can easily switch my consciousness from the current avatar to the other avatars, becoming thus a voyager, a shapeshifter, a traveler between worlds, one who has many lives and many dreams, one who may become one through the experience of the multiplicity of universes.

C3ᴇⵜⵜⵜⵜⵜ

There are seven types of avatar one can have. Each of these bodies corresponds to seven planes of existence where the dreamer can have experiences.

The first avatar is the organic body. This is the vehicle we have manifested to be able to have experiences in the physical plane. The organic body obtains data through the senses and, with that, creates the simulation we experience. It is important to understand that, without an organic body, we would not be able to experience the world as we do, because we need this organic brain, and the senses attached to it, to create the simulation.

The organic body is, at the same time, the alchemical furnace where the higher bodies can be created. Without the organic body, we would not be able to produce the substances necessary to build higher bodies. The organic body is both the generator and the blue print for the formation of the etheric and the astral bodies. It is the organic body that generates the subtle substances that feed the etheric body. Once the etheric body is fully formed, having become fully detachable from the organic, it can also generate even finer substances used in the formation of the astral body.

When we build the etheric body, we pattern its form after the architecture of the organic body, and in this way, we create a vehicle that can perceive the etheric plane as the organic body perceives through the senses. This allows us to travel in the etheric body though the etheric plane, which is very close to the physical plane and resembles it.

Since the structure of the ethereal body resembles the organic body in shape and function, this ethereal body also can create a body made of astral light. The astral body becomes then a vehicle for the consciousness to travel through the different layers of the astral plane.

The organic, etheric, and astral bodies are the first three of seven possible bodies we can create. These three are the ones we need to travel in the physical and the astral planes. Higher bodies are possible, and their formation constitute, as far as the lower three bodies are concerned, the creation of an immortal soul.

These four higher bodies are: the body of light, which is a body of solar consciousness intimately connected to our True Self; the causal body, which is a body that holds our pure will and is endowed with the power of magick and able to accomplish what we came to do in this incarnation; the body of habits, which holds the key to conscious incarnation, has conscious remembrance of our past lives, and unifies the Dreaming and waking into one single consciousness; and finally, the Essence, or angelic body, which is the vehicle of pure divine presence, capable of existing in the highest realms possible for our consciousness.

The organic body is the key to our evolution. Without it, no higher body would be possible. As E.J. Gold says, "It is a terrible waste of the opportunity of human life, a genuine sin, to have failed to use the human biological machine for our possible evolution."[1]

We are now ready to develop our dream avatar into a fully functional etheric body.

---

1 Gold, E.J., *The Human Biological Machine as a Transformational Apparatus.* Pg. 24

The Etheric Body

Let us begin with a simple realization about the nature of things. I want you to understand at this moment that the universe you perceive—everything that you perceive visually, aurally, sensorially, and olfactorily—is perceived because it is a vibration. That's an easy enough concept to understand. Everything that you perceive is vibration. You only perceive vibration. Vibration is perceived through your nervous system. There is nothing in this physical universe that you can perceive without your nervous system receiving and transmitting vibration. Therefore, you must understand that the whole universe, as you perceive it at this moment, is your nervous system. The light that hits your eye is vibration. It is vibration that enters your nervous system and your brain decodes it. Every sound is perceived by your ear drums and sent to the brain through the nervous system.

In addition, the brain adds to the received data whatever is necessary to transform our perceptions into a three-dimensional analog universe. The universe is not received by the senses in the way we recreate it in our brains. Colors and three-dimensional depth are inside your brain. Color is not a feature of the outside world. What the eyes receive are impressions of light with different rates of vibration. Our brain interprets these packets of light and uses the information contained therein to create, in our consciousness, perceptions of color and shade. The colors we perceive are not out there in the real world, they are inside our brains, created by our brains to give us a color coded world. In the same way, our eyes do not receive images in three dimensions. What the eye perceives is a two-dimensional image. The brain takes the images impressed in both eyes and codes the images into bioelectric packets that are sent through neural synapses to the brain. The brain, then, takes this information and recreates the perception of depth using the differences between the images in both eyes, adding shade and color to create a more useful representation of the world around us.

We are constantly creating this three- dimensional hallucination, where we project ourselves by also creating a three-dimensional body within the environment we are simulating.

ॐ ॐ

So, look at it now. Perceive it: this room, the sounds around, the humming of the refrigerator, the light that touches everything around, and everything you can perceive through the skin on your body.

ॐ ॐ

Know, also, that everything you perceive is inside you. That doesn't mean there is nothing outside you. There is plenty outside, as well; but this thing that you are perceiving, this thing called physical reality, is simply how you perceive your nervous system. This is your nervous system perceiving yourself. **This, your actual experience right now as you read this page, is the brain perceiving the brain.** And when I say *the brain*, I mean not just the gray mass in your head, but also its extension: the entire physical body. This complex system called *the body* is a reflection of the universe, it is the universe as we perceive it.

Look around you and feel everything. Know that everything is being perceived inside you. It is as if you have this membrane that you cannot normally perceive, and inside of this membrane, inside of this bubble, is the universe. This bubble is yourself. And this universe you perceive now, with its infinite space, unending time, stars, plants, animals, friends, is all inside you. Of course, there are things outside this membrane as well. So that whatever you're perceiving inside is the result of something hitting the membrane, something pushing on the membrane, something showering on the membrane. And you don't perceive that which is outside directly nor the membrane itself. You don't perceive it, at least, when your attention is on the phenomenal perception of the inner universe. You mostly only perceive it as it is inside. Once you understand this, you can let go of the annoying question that comes up that says, "Is this really happening or is it in my head? "The answer is always *yes*. This is really happening, and it is only in your head.

So you have this mysterious membrane that is almost never seen, seldom perceived, and that is receiving the impressions from the outside universe. Inside, it is creating this universe that you can perceive. And somewhere inside this universe, you have created an image of yourself. This image, we call *the physical body*. It is an avatar that we use to change what we see, what we hear, and our location in space and time. We let it have a run for a time period we call *a lifetime* in order to be able to perceive this universe from this particular point of view. When that lifetime is over, everything has to be rearranged when a new bubble is put in place and a new lifetime is taken. **Every new born child is a new universe, a new rearrangement of the effects of the infinite showering its light on a new membrane.**

This physical body is put together from the same vibrational stuff that the universe is made of. The phenomenal universe is made of vibration. Vibration is energy. Everything around you is energy. There is no difference between physical matter and energy. Everything is vibration, and everything is energy. Even the organic body, put together to perceive the universe, is energy, vibration. It moves. It vibrates. Which means that it comes into existence, and it ends. All the time moving, ending. Moving, ending. Quickly. Rapidly. Before you can realize that it's ending, it's over.

But that which pervades the vibrational wave, that invisible and imperceptible consciousness that makes spirit vibrate, keeps moving from one vibrational wave to the next. The intelligence that keeps experiencing the ending of the vibration keeps putting it together. Everything is vibration. Therefore everything is energy. What, then, makes up this organic body? It is, at its root, vibration. It is a consciousness that uses the energy around it. This is the Noumenal Self, beyond phenomenal appearance. This Noumenal Self rides the waves of existence, of phenomenal existence, experiencing life and the ending of life. It moves from one lifetime to another, and even at this instant, it is riding the waves of manifested energy; therefore, its phenomenal body is, at all moments, being created and destroyed without itself ever being created or destroyed. **Your Noumenal Self is the source of the flame of your existence. It is the invisible being that burns the oxygen and that consumes the material it feeds on, creating the flame of the fire. The flame is a process, not a material thing. So is your life a process, and not a thing made up of the building blocks of life. This is why life cannot be studied as we study the molecules and material things, because the flame of life is what we, as Noumenal Selves, are using as the fuel that burns. The body is the candle that burns through the lifetime, the oxygen is the spirit energy that we call life, and the flame is the soul that we call the being, the Self, the dream self that lives and experiences throughout this lifetime. Invisible and eternal, the Noumenal Self**

is the one that makes the flame burn and who moves from flame to flame, clothed with the radiance of the flame.

You are, even now, putting together energy around you and calling it your body. Without this energy you have no body, just like without energy there is no universe. The energy that makes up, creates, moves and controls your body is called *prana*. Prana is the great spirit concentrated all around you. What is *you*? We'll get back to this many times, but *you* in this sense means that center of consciousness, that particular point of view we are calling the Noumenal Self. You are not your body. You are not your mind. **Your eternal self, existing from dream to dream and from lifetime to lifetime, is simply the point of view around which you have gathered together this pocket of energy that you perceive as your organic body.** This body you have is just energy, and everything that's perceived outside of it is being reflected inside.

This energy, prana, comes from the same place that all energy comes. Every time that you see energy moving, changing, you can realize that there is a generator of energy, a dynamo from where the energy is expanding. When we look around us, it is easy to see the biggest source of energy. Where is this energy coming from? What is the biggest generator of energy? We've looked throughout the ages, and we can only come to one conclusion: it is the sun. This sun, moment after moment, day after day, aeon after aeon, keeps radiating this tremendous amount of energy; and this is the energy our planet uses to create the world. **So we, as individual points of view, come to this planet, gather together a strong packet of energy, form an organic body, and then create a universe inside it, which we call the world. This is how we create the Tonal.**

The body moves, the heart beats, the muscles contract and expand, the bones harden and grow—slowly but strongly. The lungs supply the body with vital life energy. The blood takes this energy, cleanses the system, and delivers the vital energy to all the cells. And all the senses, at the same time, receive and codify energy. Everything you perceive is energy, and your physical body is energy itself. So, there is no true separation between the physical body and energy. They are the same. **The physical body is an expression of energy. If you understand that, you understand, then, that you already have access to your etheric body, because the etheric body is a vehicle of energy that we have put together to move about this Earth.** To go from this room to the next room, to carry me from yesterday to today and maybe tomorrow if I don't mess things up too badly, I move in this body of energy first, and it directs and controls the physical body.

Consider, for example, how you move your arm. Go ahead and lift your arm, or move any other part of your body if lifting your arm is not possible at this moment. What makes the body move? You, of course, but how? See, you *know* how to move it, but you don't know *how* you move it. Sure, you can provide a scientific explanation of how the muscles contract in response to nervous signals sent from the brain, but even then, you don't really know how that happens. What makes the nerve cells obey your intent? What makes the muscle cells respond to the impulses of the neurons? The mechanical aspects of this movement can be studied and understood, but at some point, we come to face the fact that you willed the arm to move, and that will initiate a chain of events that resulted in the arm moving. The body, if it is working properly and the channels that connect its different parts are not damaged, will respond to your will.

But there is a magical link between your conscious will and the mechanisms of your body; this link is the etheric body.

CRITICAL

I want you to place your attention on your body for a moment. In placing your attention there and withdrawing it from everything else outside of the body, you give yourself permission to dim the lights that illuminate the universe so that, for a brief moment, you're not spending a lot of energy recreating the universe. Forget for a moment, also, what you think you know about your physical body; and simply feel it, know it, and become acquainted with it in its pure state of energy. It's really simple. All you have to do is feel the body as energy. Do this at the same time that you read these words. Your attention is simply split, using a portion of it to read and understand these words, and another portion to feel the body. Use your ordinary, regular attention. No need to use imagination or any special ability. Simply let the body feel itself, perceive itself as energy. You will realize that the shape you imagine the body to have is not quite exactly the same as the shape of the energy body. It kind of follows similar patterns, but you perceive more concentrated energy, denser forms of this energy in some parts and more diffused energy in other parts. That is okay because that is changeable. Notice, for example, where the two or three biggest concentrations of energy are right now. Now, go ahead and diminish one of those and make one of the others bigger, stronger, more concentrated. You do that by putting your attention where you want the energy to go. Just put your attention there. Now you're going to expand it again. Make it grow, make it take the form that you imagine your physical body to have. Distribute it evenly.

Now, notice that there are a few small pockets that have little or no energy. Just take a deep breath and fill them up. The energy coming through the breath goes wherever you want it to go. Try it. Fill out those pockets. Now, keep breathing and keep sending the prana that comes through every part, just like waves of the ocean crashing on

71

the beach. Notice that as you do this, you're filling up your etheric body with fresh, clear vibrations. This is true breathing. This is how the energy coming through the sun creates your physical body. If you place your attention on one of your hands, a lot of the energy rushes to that hand. Try it. Now this hand is fuller and bigger than the other hand. Switch it. Place your attention on the other hand and breath into it. Now make them even. Send it to both at the same time. Notice how they vibrate and balance.

Now, place the attention on your heart center. Notice the energy body concentrated there. Notice how it tends to clump around the center of your attention. This is your energy body, your etheric body. Now, move that center of attention, which means move yourself down, down to your second chakra. Notice that the energy there has a different expression of vibration than when it is in your heart. It rests comfortably there, in between your belly button and your genitals. You can breath into it. Charge it. Now, expand it again. Breathe into it and allow it to balloon up to cover the shape of the body. You concentrate it by breathing in, you expand it by breathing out. Take a few more breaths. Expand your energy body until it fits the image of your physical body like a glove. Now, look around you and notice that the vibration of your body is reflected in the vibration of the world around you.

CʒໞໞCʒໞ

This is your body of energy. This is your etheric body. You will see that this etheric body can be used to heal, to grow, and also to move. When we concentrate it as the physical body, we move from one place to another on this physical earth. But it is also possible to concentrate this as pure energy and move as energy throughout the physical world. It is simple. It is easy. The only thing that stands in the way is the mind. Because the mind and the imagination create the world around. Or rather, it is used to create the way the world is perceived. You move, and that's easy. But when the mind says, "No, you're not moving," then you don't perceive yourself as moving. But you will do it because it's really easy to do. And it's within your power to do. I will show you how. And then, you'll be able to use this etheric body to travel on this earth as you will—to move, to visit and to perceive as you will.

Try the following experiment:

CB☙ನ☚BꝎ

Take a comfortable posture. Put the tip of your tongue on the roof of your mouth. Begin by removing your social mask by slowly drawing the tips of your fingers across your face in a downward stroke, from top to bottom. Repeat this a few times; and every time you do that, relax the facial muscles. There are a lot of tiny muscles on your face designed to create an expression. Right now, no one is watching you, so take off that mask. There will be a sensation of light, or air, or light air where your face usually is, and that is when you know you have taken it off. Now, breathe in and out slowly, purposefully, and feel the energy around the center of your attention. Every time you breathe in, the etheric body strengthens, and when you breathe out, it cleanses. Breathe in. Breathe out. What you breathe in is prana, pure energy. This energy, this vibration, is what you utilize to form a body. At this moment, you don't need to create a physical body. It is already formed. But you can surround yourself with this ball of energy. Now, you will feel a slight pull ahead of you, in the direction in which you hold the book. It's pulling towards a point beyond the book in front of you. You feel this energy that you have created being attracted, pulled. Stay at the center of the energy. It's okay to just feel the pull. Now, while you feel this pull, begin to form a copy of your body. Use your imagination to create a replica of your body. The pull, the magnetic force that pulls you, should be at the center of this body. Use your imagination to give form to this etheric body. It is an imaginary copy. See your shoulders, your arms, your head, legs, torso, neck. Imagine the eyes of your etheric body still closed. Your energy is infusing this body that you are creating in your imagination. Now breathe in, allowing the energy to grow, and breathe out. In a few moments, you will close your physical eyes. When that happens, you will find yourself just a few inches in front of the sitting physical body. Realize at that moment that the physical body is just a memory, an image. You always find yourself at the center of a ball of energy that you are now shaping into a body that looks like yours, but it's standing. This body standing—know it to be you. You will be standing in this same room. Keep breathing in. Breathe out. This body you have just created has a face, has eyes, hands, feet. Open the eyes of your etheric body and just let any impression come to your mind. It doesn't matter if it's mental or not. Open your etheric eyes. See the room. Look at the center of the room and see that force that is touching you with its tendrils. Look around you and see everyone else. See how the room is different and how it's similar to the room you remember. Breathe into this body of light and breathe out. Take a step or two closer to the center, to that ball of energy in front of you. Don't go all the way. Just a few steps. Look around one more time. Now, slowly move back to where you were sitting before. Sit down again in the same posture in which you started the exercise. Feel yourself merging into the physical body.

Now, close your eyes and experience what you just read and more. When you are back, keep reading.

Now, breathe. Notice that the magnetic pull is no longer active. Allow your etheric body to sink into the form of the physical. Take another deep breath, and allow the energy to infuse the form of the physical and fit into it like a glove. Take one more deep breath and you'll feel healthy, awake and strong.

CS℘CR℘

Take a few moments to notate your experience in your journal.

CS℘CR℘

The etheric body is force and energy that you have gathered around you; the you that has no dimensions, no body, nothing other than a point of reference: presence and attention. This pranic force is always present when you move your hands, when you walk, when you see, when you speak or anything else that you do. It is where you magically exert the force of your will so that you may do something in this world. It comes from the force of your etheric body.

This same force allows you to move out of the physical body and move about the Earth. It is not that it moves out of the body, it's simply that it's forming the body, moving the body, but it can also move without the physical body. **It is a force that has been with you since birth. We call it the *daemon*, the *other self*, the *ally*. It is the familiar spirit of a sorcerer. It is elemental in nature. It is made of that force that flows through the sun and that is composed of akasha, a spiritual force, and manifests as the four elements.**

Your etheric body is an elemental. What kind of elemental? That depends on the moment of your birth. Because it is at the moment

75

of your birth that you gather the energies around you to shape around the physical body being born. So, it depends on your birth sign. Is it water, fire, earth, air? Whatever was predominant at that moment, that's the strength of your etheric body. But it contains all the other elements too. It is only that its primary force is equivalent to the predominant force around you at the moment of your birth.

You have a very intimate knowledge and connection to this elemental because it has been your body, your container, all your life. It has been always there with you. You hear its thoughts as if they were your thoughts. It hears everything that you say and knows everything that you want. But it has its own wants as well, because it is an elemental. It is attached to you. You are the center of its existence. That point of view that is your true self, your ego, is in an evolutionary stage above the elemental that accompanies you through life, and so you are to it as your Holy Guardian Angel is to you. It doesn't have the stellar presence that is behind your own center. You belong to a higher plane of existence, higher than the elemental plane. And so, it attaches to you, serves you as your vehicle, your avatar, in this physical plane. It is the horse and you are the rider of the horse. This is true, not only of the physical body, it is also true of the elemental, the etheric double. It has been carrying you all your life, manifesting this physical body for you to move in this dimension. It does the same thing when you move in the lower parts of the astral plane. It can take you anywhere that has a physical elemental presence, a physical elemental vibration. In other words, it can take you anywhere on this planet.

To know all these aspects of it allows you to communicate and to enable it to do more things for you.

The magician can acquire more servants like this, more familiars. There is a point when you need to have command over four elementals. But your own etheric body is always an elemental, too, so it can take many shapes and many functions. It is capable of retrieving information and bringing it to you. It is capable of doing things for you. It is also capable of deceiving you—giving you what you want, not what you need. But it is tricky, too. It can make you fall by fooling you into only pursuing your wants and not your will. It's looking for experience and vibration because it is made of vibration. So it wants food, drugs, drinks, sex, laughter, sorrow, drama. It wants money. It wants this and that. And it knows what you want in your heart. It is important to learn to maneuver it, to detach it from the physical form, to learn to separate so that more work can happen after the limits of the physical form. This *more work* that can happen after the physical death has its basis on the fact that it can operate as an etheric double because, as an etheric double, it moves on the lower part of the astral plane, free from the constraints placed on the ordinary organic body. This is just the bottom of the astral plane. From here, you begin to build a body that is made with the material of the higher planes. This astral body will allow you to travel to the higher planes.

How to Construct the Astral Body

Here's the manner in which to achieve the construction of the astral body, which is the key to deeper and higher explorations of the Dreaming and the astral plane.

Everything that you perceive through the five senses is vibration. This vibration is energy that is alive and conscious. As such, you are surrounded at all times by consciousness and life. Whether the objects around you appear to be inert or unconscious, they are very much alive, vibrant, and have their own degree of consciousness. Our own bodies are constructed of molecules and atoms that are also vibration. Everything phenomenal, therefore, is part of this ocean of life, consciousness, and vibration. The astral plane and the Dreaming are, in themselves, part of this ocean. They are gateways to the vastness of the ocean. Your organic body, your vehicle, is a concentration of vibratory forces that your consciousness utilizes to move about this world. This body was created using the genetic blueprint of your DNA.

Ultimately, the body itself is a living, conscious aggregate that constitutes, in itself, the outermost manifestation of your consciousness.

Every part of you, from the highest spiritual essence to your psyche, your mind, your emotional body, your dream self and your organic body, is a layer of your spiritual consciousness. Just like you created the organic body, it is possible to create other vehicles that would allow you to operate, to exist and to manipulate more refined and subtle planes of existence. The key is to remember that the organic body is composed, or put together, from the vibratory building blocks around us; from the same vibrational stuff that the world itself is composed of. That which directs the formation, the maintenance and, ultimately, the dissolution of your organic body is a very old intelligence, one that existed long before the beginning of civilization, long before your identity was formed. But, just like this body has been put together from vibration, we can also form another body made up of a more subtle vibration: the vibration of the astral plane.

Everything that we perceive through any of the senses is vibration, it is life and it is consciousness. As we perceive it, it is the densest form of vibration and the densest form of consciousness. This is life. With the mind—the conscious mind, which is a more subtle and inner layer of our consciousness than the body—we can direct the construction of this astral body. We use the blueprint of the vehicle we already possess: the physical self. We create a twin with the mind, with the imagination, with our visualization. This twin is an identical copy of the organic body. You will dress in accordance to the space or the chamber you want to visit. This is no different than creating a dream avatar. For, every time you go to sleep and find yourself in a dream, you have created, out of your own imagination, a dream body that can navigate that space. The only difference is that the dream self is created automatically and unconsciously out of the psychic material that exists in our subconscious at that time. But now, we are to create a dream self or an astral body by conscious means.

ॐ ॐ ॐ ॐ

Visualization and imagination give your astral body form, shape. They gather astral light around themselves to create this vehicle. So,

80

you begin by sitting down or laying down, relaxing and getting your consciousness to that liminal stage: the threshold space. And there, in that threshold between the waking and the Dreaming, you see next to you, or in front of you, or behind you, or above you, the doppelgänger, the twin. Practice visualizing it as many times as you can. Visualize it when you're not sleeping. Visualize it when you're falling asleep. Visualize it when you can see. The more you visualize it, the quicker this body will be formed.

C3ℰ0Cℛℰ0

This body, like any other body, needs more than a form. It needs substance. The substance of this body is light: the light of the astral plane. And with this, I will tell you a secret that has existed in many esoteric traditions around the world. The astral light inside the human body is life itself, and the sexual force is the concentration and source of this light. Therefore, to give life to this astral body, you need to infuse it with your life. You feed the astral body with your vibrations. You feed it with your emotions. You feed it with your attention. You feed it with your chi, with your etheric energy. And you feed it with your sexual desire.

I will give you a practical exercise you can follow. Read it first to fully understand how to do it, then follow the instructions when you are ready:

C3ℰ0Cℛℰ0

Sit in a comfortable position and imagine behind you a body of light identical to your organic body. Dress it in white. With your eyes closed, try to see this twin self in detail. Look at the hair, the shape of the nose, the thickness of the neck. Look at the fingernails, the shape of the feet. See this twin with its eyes closed. Now you're going to infuse it with your light. See yourself filled with the light of your own consciousness and send light from you to the twin. Now, take a deep breath and hold it for a moment; you will receive an extra shock of energy. Now, see the double glowing stronger. Allow your point of view to move from the center of your head to the center of the head of the astral body. Open the eyes of the astral body and see the back of your head in front of you. See where you're sitting. See the room around you. Now, gently close your eyes and consciously take the shape of your organic body. Occupy the space of your organic body. Penetrate the organic body by adopting its posture. Then, remain in this state, feeling the vibrations that your astral body brought with it. That concludes this exercise.

೮౩ ೭ಾ ೧౭ ೮౦

Feel now all around you, all around your body, the presence of this astral body. See how, when you breathe, light is transferred to it. When you eat, be conscious of the fact that you are also feeding the astral body with the light that exists in the form of food. And when you feel sexual arousal, especially when you are by yourself, know that the more intense the sexual arousal, the more life and substance you are giving to this astral body.

೮౩ ೭ಾ ೧౭ ೮౦

To completely and consciously develop the ability to detach your astral body from your organic body, you must feed it with your sexual force. You do this by stimulating your sexual force until it fills the astral body. It is important for the male to be able to do this for long periods of time without ejaculating, because the orgasm in the male and the formation of semen depletes the body from this astral force, from this astral light. To feed the astral body properly, a man must learn to maintain this exercise for over an hour and to do so with purity in his heart and a spiritual aspiration in his mind. For a female, the formula works differently. The more and stronger the orgasms she achieves, the more she feeds her astral body. She must learn to do this with a pure heart, a heart that aspires to God and a mind that is silent. It is with the employment of this formula that you may create an astral body that can travel independently of the organic body, that can go anywhere in the Dreaming to witness, to learn and to experience.

C3ᔕᗡᏟᏕᏴᎧ

By using a formula of flying through the aethers, one can also learn to go above and beyond the astral plane into higher and more subtle planes of existence for one's evolution, for one's initiation, and for the benefit of All Beings Everywhere.

Advanced Shamanic Techniques

I was preparing to give a weekend workshop on astral mastery. As usual, a lot of dreaming and information was coming in as I was making my preparations. The night before the workshop, I had a dream of power. It was one of those dreams where a lot of things seem to be happening at the same time, and whatever I was engaged in seemed to be going on, and on, and on. The students and I were preparing the space for the weekend. We had some tables set up outside by the front porch, where the community was working. There was this one point that kept coming to my mind. It was a recurrent loop. The same thing would happen over and over. The last time it happened was when I realized that this was something I needed to pay attention to. I was sitting outside, on the front porch of the group house, on a rocking chair. I was thinking about how well the workshop was going. Then I said, "Maybe one day we should have a workshop for shamans." A group of my students came out then, and I told them I was thinking that I should give a workshop for shamans that can voyage. Then, my brother Carlos stopped and, looking at me, said, "Yeah, but then E.J. would do this," and he opened his mouth wide. His mouth got round and I could see something inside that was like a wall. Inside this wall there was a hole of light. There was a strange sound coming out of it and a strange thing happening inside. It was funny in the visceral-belly-laugh kind of funny. At the same time, the opening of the mouth was a true gateway to another reality. It reminded me of the doorway shown in the Shadow Walk video shot in Teotihuacan, where I'm shadow walking with Eric De La Para, and one can see the presence of the Nahual through it. At that moment, when Carlos opened his mouth wide in the dream, I saw the Nahual, too. I remembered that I had seen this, in this very same dream, many times; that this dream has been happening many times; and that, every time, Carlos makes this joke about E.J., where he opens his mouth and the Nahual peeks back through it.[2]

I realized that in this chapter about astral mastery, I am to open the mouth of the Nahual and let it come through. So, it is meant to be a chapter for shamans.

By now, you may have come to realize that, in this book, we make little emphasis on the distinction between the inner and the outer worlds. That is, we have heretofore treated all experience as a dream, and we have set aside the question of whether a particular experience can be considered to be happening inside the mind or if it can be said that it is occurring outside of ourselves. It is not that the distinction is meaningless, but it is malleable and, as such, it is subject to be seen as one or the other, or both, at the convenience of the practitioner. Whether an experience is seen as happening outside the mind or inside the mind, or even outside or inside the body, depends on what model of the universe we are using. Bishop Berkeley claimed that the entire universe was inside the mind. To avoid solipsism, he refused to believe that it was all inside his own human mind, but rather within the mind of God. **If we take this view, then we can say that each one of us is a point of view of that Absolute that sleeps and dreams, the being the Hindus call Brahma; and each of us, being a particular dream of that infinite mind, is inside a dream and is, indeed, part of that dream.**

On the other hand, we could take a more modern point of view and refuse to accept any terms that cannot be proven by science and, thus, refuse to accept obscure categories like "mind," unless

1 See the publications section of www.koyotetheblind.com for a copy of *Shadow Walk* and other videos.

it can be scientifically proven that it has an existence outside the brain. Let us, then, consider the possibility that all the experiences and techniques, here presented, are only part of the neural network of our nervous system, and nothing we are doing happens outside the body. In this case, we still come to the same conclusion: that we are always in a dream. That's because, whether we are talking about having a dream, doing a conscious voyage up into the higher planes, or simply going outside to tend to our garden, we are experiencing a world created by the reaction of our neural network to whatever waves and electromagnetic fields impinge upon said neural network. **In other words, whether we think of our experience as being outside the body or only happening within the brain, we have to come to the same conclusion, and that is that we are in the midst of an experience that is being arranged and codified according to some unconscious principles. We are always in a dream, and we are always interpreting the nature of that dream.**

Therefore, the question of whether we are outside the body or experiencing the magical and shamanic practices within the body can always be answered with a *yes*.

However—and this is a very crucial point if you hope to get to a higher level of attainment in these practices—the fact still remains that there is a qualitative distinction in our experience of an event, in terms of its objectivity. We can philosophize about the subjective nature of every experience until we are blue in the face playing the flute in the Ganges river surrounded by milk maidens, but that won't change the fact that some experiences feel "objectively real" and others feel "like it was a dream. "That distinction itself is also part of our experience. Some experiences seem to have more reality density than others, and the impact they have on our consciousness, and even in our eternal being, depends on their density.

It is possible, therefore, to gain control of how deeply we can be affected by an experience by making the faculty of discrimination, which allows us to feel the "reality" of an experience, conscious. While this judgment is made unconsciously by most, it is the purview of the shaman and the magician to make this faculty voluntary and conscious. The trick is in being able to decide how real and relevant an experience is and, in that manner, deciding how much attention and personal power to invest in it. **The more importance we give to an event, the more objectively real it seems to be and, therefore, the more of an impact it has on us. This is the esoteric meaning behind the term** *paying attention.*

In general, we use the organic and etheric bodies as vehicles to navigate and experience in the realm we have classified as "external," and the astral and etheric bodies, we use to go within and experience the inner planes of existence. However, these inner planes are not merely subjective. There is a point where they actually acquire a deeper and more meaningful level of objectivity and reality, to the point where all other experiences below that plane seem like they were fleeting and unreal, like a dream of existence that fades in comparison to the stark and naked reality of the higher realms. Don't be quick, therefore, to decide what is subjective and what is objective. In each case, an experience carries with it such a distinction, and the experienced shaman and magician knows how to apply such a discriminating judgment in order to command and operate the degree of influence an experience will have in her essential and eternal being.

In fact, to say that your organic body stays and your etheric body goes into the world is only one way to say it. Because what stays, in truth, is only your memory of having an organic body. And as long as you're remembering that organic body sitting there in your chair or laying in bed, it is simply that part of your attention being used to keep that form. You have, at that moment, a dislocated and bi-located presence. A little bit of it is in the organic body, and a little bit of it is in the etheric, but they're both convenient and useful constructs of our consciousness. In truth, when you're voyaging, you don't even need an organic body. You can drop it altogether from your attention for a moment and get it back when you seek to return. **And, in fact, although it's harder to do because it's harder to master the attention at this level, the physical can be recreated anywhere. It is only a manifestation of the etheric. And that's why sometimes you can be in two different places at once and even move between worlds, realities, and time tracks.**

In practices that are beyond the scope of this book, you can learn to move into other worlds—some not quite human at all. **You can voyage, even, with your organic body to other realms of existence and move from this universe to a parallel one, where the socio-political realities are different than what you believe to be real.** While this sounds like a far-fetched claim to many, the truth of it can be easily demonstrated. I have been able to take other individuals, and even small groups, to different time tracks and different places on this Earth by shifting between the worlds with the organic body. This ability is the effect of intense and dedicated work with the principles and exercises in this book, but admittedly, it takes many lifetimes to master the process.

A much easier ability to master is voyaging in the etheric body through the lower astral plane, where the world seems just as real as the physical world. In fact, it is; but while it is just as real, it is not identical to it. **The world we experience in the etheric body is, in truth, a link between the astral and the physical, and it contains its own set of objects and beings.** As far as being real, however, it is just as real as the physical and, in fact, has a tremendous effect on the physical. Everything that exists in the physical world has a counterpart in the etheric plane. Changes in one can affect the other. Much information can be obtained this way.

The next ability that is accessible to all of us is that of learning to consciously voyage in the astral body. This is a more internal experience, at first. Very much like conscious dreaming, it uses imagination and begins with a voluntary form of day dreaming, as we have seen in previous chapters. However, with experience, we come to see that astral voyaging does not stay in the willed imagination, which is truly just a gateway to the higher planes.

Shapeshifting is a powerful and very useful skill to learn. It truly accomplishes what the Toltecs called *losing the form*. The reason we are so bound to the physical world and even to the Tonal (the human world co-created by all of us) is that we have not exercised the practice of shapeshifting and have come to believe that we are limited by the form we have learned to take. **In other words, we have programmed ourselves into the form we have (physical and mental), and have forgotten how to become.**

CʒꙄꙄꙄꙄ

You become other things in dreams because the etheric double can take any shape and also appear as different things or take the body of other animals. This etheric body takes the shape of your organic body. It kind of infuses it. It is possible to see an animal—your pet, your cat, your fish, your eagle—and put your consciousness into it. That means that you can put your etheric body there and take it's form and direct it as if it was your body, see what it sees and do what it does. It is a weird experience because the animal, for a moment, loses itself and feels possessed by you. Some animals will welcome it as a possibility for their evolution. But you can also just take that form, if your clarity of mind allows you to do so, or you can have no-form manifested in the physical and simply move as etheric form.

⚔⚔⚔

Everything is energy and everything moves. Everything vibrates. The organic body is the denser form of vibration that we're manifesting. Therefore, it is slower. To go from where you are now to the backyard of your home, you need to move your body, getup, go out, and go to the backyard. It takes time and physical effort to move the organic body, for it has to follow the laws of the world it belongs to. **Or, in gaming terms, the avatar follows the laws of its environment because it is an intrinsic part of it; both, avatar and its environment, are part of the same program. To do the same in the etheric body, you can travel with the speed of thought— move from here to there or anywhere on this planet.** And it takes as much effort and as much speed to go to the backyard as it does to go to Spain, to San Francisco, to Argentina. The organic body is a buffer. It slows down the process. At the same time, it's receiving all the physical experience of the physical world. The etheric body has its own senses. The etheric world is received with such clarity of touch, of smell, of sound, of sight, because it is the outer layer of the being. The etheric body is an elemental, and as such, it is not bound by this outer layer of the organic. It is manifesting this outer layer. **So, when you travel in the etheric body, it's only your thought or your expectation that's slowing you down.**

It's really that and nothing more that makes you think:

Well, I'm still in my body.

I can't get out.
I can get out, but I don't know if it's my imagination.

Yeah, I can see that I'm here, somewhere else, but I still feel my body, so maybe I'm just dreaming.

All of that mind chatter is simply the thing that's slowing you down. All you really need is to desire something—to *will* something, to be more clear. Will to be somewhere, and the etheric body will take you there. Everything else that the mind does—the reasons for the *because* and the *what-ifs*—is simply slowing you down, keeping you from seeing, keeping you from moving. If you will it, it will do it for you. It will carry you. No different than when I will to see what is to my left: all I have to do is allow my body to give me what I will, which is to turn and look. If I want to get water, I get up and go. My body obeys. Why? Because it is infused with the etheric body whose function is to obey my will. **So it is with your etheric body. You will something and it will do it for you. You can slow it down with your thoughts, your expectations and your doubts, but it will do it. Just let it do it.**

We're going to do an exercise now.

ॐ৩৹৻৩ঌ

This time, you're going to come out of the body and you're going to go somewhere. Take a moment to decide where you're going to go and write

92

it down. Say it in the present tense. Say, "I am going to…," and name the place—anywhere on this planet and anywhere in this dimension. When you have written it down, read the instructions below. When you have understood the instructions, close your eyes and do the exercise.

Place the tip of your tongue on the roof of your mouth. Take a deep breath. Feel your etheric body vibrate stronger as you breathe. As the prana fills it, feel the vibration all around your skin. Continue breathing prana into it. Feel yourself growing a few inches above and around your physical form. Grow just a little bit more, until you feel yourself in a bubble of light roughly with the shape of your physical form. Notice your organic body still inside you. Your organic body, as others see it, is now inside you, smaller than you. Notice how it begins to fade into your light. Now you are this body of energy. Allow the remnants of the organic to dissolve into you. It will be back. Just leave it there for a moment. Now, see in front of you a doorway. You feel its subtle pull. You can hear it. Feel its hum. You will go through that door to the place of your choosing. When you see what you went there to see, you will come back. Now, go and experience. When you are done, or when you feel your attention getting distracted, drifting into dreams or getting tired, come back.

Now, remember where you came from and go back there. Simply decide to go back. See your body where you left it. Look around you one more time. Feel the radiation, the light emanating from the center of the room. Breathe in and allow it to fill you with its energy. Take the form and shape of your organic body. Sink into it. Adopt its shape and its form. Take another deep breath. Slowly open your eyes. Take a few moments to write down your experience.

CREDACRED

We're going to work a little more with the etheric body, and we're going to come outside the body. We're going to go up and anywhere in this plane, this planet. This time, what you are going to be doing is looking for an animal or plant, any kind of animal or plant. You're going to ask permission to enter its body. Then, you're going to enter that body and experience it. If the *guardian* or the brother[2] says *no*, then look for another one.

C33ᴤꝅᴒ

Get into a comfortable position and close your eyes. Place the tip of your tongue on the roof of your mouth. Find a place at the center of your head from where all thoughts emanate. Notice that it is surrounded by energetic vibration, by a "stuff" made of vibration, light, sound. Feed it and strengthen it with every breath you take. At some point, you'll feel a slight pull from the center of the room. Remember at this point to relax your face. Next, allow the etheric double to stand. Let it stand in front of where you are sitting. Form the body as a copy of your organic body. Notice the doorway in front of you, in the center of the room. Open your etheric eyes. When it's time, cross that doorway. Once you get to where you're going, look for an animal, a plant or a tree. Ask permission when you see it. When permission is given, enter and go with the experience inside of that other body.

Now, if you feel tired or feel the body of the animal stressing out, come back. Otherwise, stay for as long as you want, provided you can maintain the attention. When you come back, begin by feeling your organic body. Come back to the room. Bring all your memories with you. Take your human form. Adopt the current posture of

---

2 In our tradition, we see all animals as our brothers, and all plants as guardians. And thus, our offerings to *All Our Relations* is equivalent to the Bodhisattva's vow for *All Sentient Beings Everywhere*.

your body. Settle into it. Take a deep breath and open your eyes. Feel the etheric body inside you. Take a moment to write down your experience.

ఇ౸౿ఴ

Place the tip of your tongue on the roof of your mouth. Take a deep breath. Feel the etheric body, vibrant, in and around your body. Know it is giving life and form to the organic body. Feed the etheric body with your breath. Take off your social mask. Move your fingers over the surface of your face. Relax every point on your face until there is only light. Now, you will feel a pull from above. Go ahead and climb. Follow that pull until you are hovering just above the place where you were sitting, floating in midair. Open the eyes of the etheric body. See the room around you. Continue to flow upwards, passing through the ceiling, the attic, the rooftop. Hover above, and then keep going up until you find yourself right at the border of the stratosphere. And there, right outside the atmosphere of the planet, fill your body with the light of the sun and the stars. When the body is full, you will remember your body down on the planet and come back. Go, and make your body get filled with the light. Go. When you come back, open your eyes and write down your experience.

ఇ౸౿ఴ

We're going to move on to the advanced practices. You're going to light a candle. Place it on your altar, if you have one, or in any safe place that can stand as an altar, for now, in your room. Then, you are going to travel up into the astral plane.

ఇ౸౿ఴ

The way to the planes, to mastery of the planes, is the following. You're going to come out of the body in your body of light. You're going to take a form, a shape, in your likeness. But you're going to have a different kind of dress. You're going to have a white robe— gold trim on the sleeves. You can add any sacred symbol that you want to it. You can come out in any of the ways we described before. When you are ready, begin to rise up. Keep your eyes closed and go up. Keep going up. Don't stop. Go up. Go up as fast as you want, and don't stop. Don't open your eyes. Just keep going up. If you feel like it's time to open your eyes, don't open them yet. Just keep going up. If you're getting tired, don't stop. Just keep going up. If you get exhausted, keep going up. Keep going up until it's impossible to go any more. At one point, you will either fall asleep or you will find yourself in a different plane of existence. Then, you explore and interact as you will.

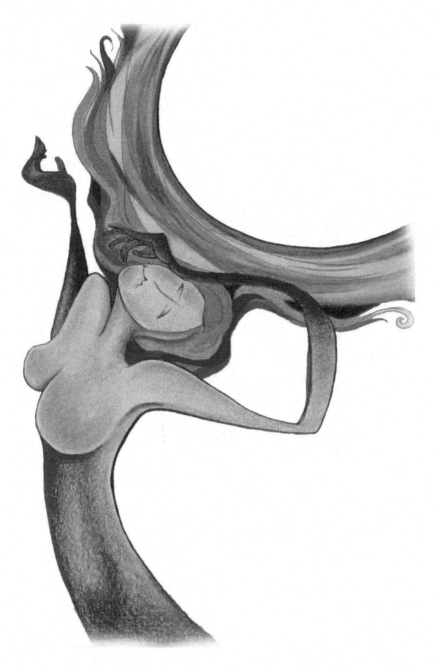

Qoph
Xochitl Flores-Jaramillo

Part III:

And in the Philosopher's Garden
Lives the Scent
of a Golden Flower.

The Beast

The Dreaming is not to be seen as just a state of consciousness. It is a being, conscious and with a life of its own. Who is the Dreaming? You will come to know the Dreaming as a beast who is always surrounding you—the one watching you. Every move you make ... recorded, observed, registered. The beast appears to you in different forms, but you can always sense it around you. You can sense it now, right on the verge of your consciousness, touching your skin. You can feel her on your face: tiny tendrils, minute, touching your forehead, surrounding your hair, supporting your weight. This beast! You can feel her forming a circle around you.

This beast, we call Dreaming. It breathes with you.

If you let your eyes just stare without fixating on anything in particular, just diffuse your vision, you will begin to get a glimpse of tiny movements in the body of this beast, Dreaming.

If you're quiet enough, you begin to feel it breathing. You can feel the walls moving. This beast is present in every dream that we have. Whether we are sleeping or waking, any time we seem to be surrounded by anything at all—a room, a field, a road, a tomb— we find ourselves surrounded by this beast. The beast, Dreaming, is the oldest creature you've ever encountered. It was here before you were born. It is there every night, and it is around you right now. It covers all empty space. It lets the light shine through its walls—filter through. The shapes of objects and their sounds come through. Yet, if you learn to pay attention, you will see the body of the beast. If you close your eyes, you will sense it with your chest, with your forearms. If you move your hands, you touch its surface; you feel the curvature of its body eternal; you feel the pockets of resistance and fluidity.

And this beast, you find everywhere. You dream, and in this dream you have experiences, and you wake up talking about and remembering the dream; but the beast we don't mention. We don't speak of her, simply because she's always been there. Yet it is a common feature of your waking life and your dreaming life. She is there always, as everything that is not *I*. Any space we enter is the body of the beast.

But make no mistake, this is no metaphor—no image. It is the most real thing around. Everything else changes. Everything else is born, lives and dies. Everything shifts. Everything vanishes. Everything. The beast remains—supple, changeable yet eternal; it's nature is the shifting itself. It is almost invisible, except for the eyes that can see. She is the most real thing around, and she is watching you every movement. Every sound, every event, it watches.

When you begin to notice that the beast is there, you know one truth: that you are not alone; that all the people who surround you, and all the animals that come and go, are just part of the dream; but the beast … the beast is always there. After death, before birth, it's there. And between one life and another, the beast awaits. This is called Dreaming.

The Dreaming is bigger than life, bigger than the wave. It's bigger than the words. It's bigger than the worries. The beast is bigger than the dream. The dream that you have, even the one called life, is nothing but the way in which you are experiencing the beast. It is your confrontation with the beast. How this confrontation will go depends on many things. It depends on

the amount and quality of your personal power. It depends on the strength of your intent. It depends on when the beast will pounce and devour you.

You will learn to see the beast. You will learn to watch and observe the beast. You will know when it's watching you, and you will learn that how you move, how you see and how much personal power you have, are the keys to knowing the beast and to engaging with the beast. The Yoga of Dreaming is an art of confrontation with the beast. And in case you haven't realized it, the beast, Dreaming, is everything that you are not. And being everything that you are not, it is your other half. The degree to which you know and perceive the beast is directly related to the degree in which you know yourself.

If you're reading this book, know one thing (and I say this to you in all seriousness): you will encounter the biggest and most dreaded animal around; one that cannot be tamed, cannot be conquered, cannot be killed; one that will devour you one day and consume you the way all dreams are consumed. It will annihilate you the way all experience is annihilated. **You will have, in this book, the encounter with the most terrifying thing and the most beautiful thing. And if, at some point, you see the beast, and the beast notices you are watching, it will begin to pay more attention to you. If you're successful in this, you will have taken the first step towards mastery—which is to say: you have to master your dreaming or it will take you away.**

Look in front of you. Look around you. Look anywhere and know the Dreaming around you. It is a vibration different than any of the others. It is a light different than visible light. It is a presence. It is *stuff*.

Feel it, not only on the surface of your skin. Feel it reaching into your body. Feel its tendrils moving (tentacle-like, worm-like), seeping into your body. Feel it touching your heart, your stomach, and your spine. Feel its fingers touching your skull, entering through the back of your head, and now gently push it out. Take a deep breath and slowly push it out, gently, without fear, gently. Take another deep breath and allow it to flow in, a little bit, and then push it out. Take it in again. Push it out.

Dream Is a Dealing with Light

As I find myself in the middle of the Dreaming, I know myself to be bombarded by an intense stream of light. It's a light that leaves no shadows, because there is nothing there to stand between myself and the light. There is just light—an infinite field of light that extends itself in all directions. Anytime I find myself in any kind of dream—which is to say, any type of experience whatsoever—I am in the middle of this vast field of light. The light, intense, with a loud silence, is so devastating that I cannot remain in any way myself in its presence. So intense is this light that I begin to forget even that *I am*. This point of consciousness, which I seem to always be calling *I*, begins to dissolve itself, and I seem to enter a state of forgetfulness, of not being. There is, I found long ago, a way to protect myself from the intensity of this relentless light—a barrier raised between me and the blinding light. It is not so much a barrier but a tweak of the imagination—an interpretation of light, a way of processing light. I break it down into slower light waves, just like a prism breaks down sunlight into a rainbow. This light that surrounds me is broken down into an endless stream of dreams and experiences. Broken down, this light becomes color, shape, form. Broken down, it becomes sound and sensation. It becomes space and time. All experience, all sound, all vision is, in a way, the way in which I am dealing with this infinite field of light.

It is completely immaterial if I call this experience *a dream*, if I call it *life*, if I call it *tragedy*, if I call it *experience*. It is completely immaterial because, in the face of the light, all else is shadow. In each case, it is I who stands in the center of this world of my creation, of this moment of experience. I experience. To understand that basic equation is to begin to grasp the task of the dreamer and to begin to understand that, to master the Dreaming is to master life, that to master experience is to master self. **There is no one there creating this experience for me other than myself. It is a constant dealing between the light and me.**

If I create this dream out of fear, fear has been, then, nothing more than the mechanism, the technique by which I am confronting this Clear Light. If I generate this dream out of the need to experience, then that is the mechanism infused in the Dreaming. What, then, is mastery over the Dreaming? It is not to be able to change this or that in this experience. It is, rather, to be able to hold myself, to open myself, to close myself. It is to be able to master myself, which is to say that I am mastering my own perception; that I master the way in which I perceive light: completely fearless, absolutely unconcerned with what will happen to me. For, what I am is just one more shadow, created to stand between the light and me. Having only the sufficient mastery of my self, I confront the light, thus creating this dream. To know how I do this is to know how I deal with this.

The mastery of the Dreaming is the mastery of self. I find myself in the middle of a dream, and I dream myself a body; as I dream myself an experience; as I dream myself a chamber, a passage; as I dream myself a life. What profit could I attain from merely changing the experience? Do I not owe it to the mastery of the moment to go beyond just changing the experience, and learn to master that perceptual apparatus which, here in the human realm, we call *the nervous system, the brain, the mind...*but which, in reality, is only this external dreaming expression of perception itself?

Who is the great sorcerer who makes the sky blue and the grass green? Is it not I who perceives it? What is blue and green if not the perception of color? What is sound if not the hearing of it?

What is, then, life if not the living of it? What is dream if not the Dreaming?

The *how* to gain this mastery is a matter of perception. It's a matter of eliminating all the shadows and confusions that come from dreaming, from experiencing. I let go of everything that externally seems to be affecting me, and I place all my attention in the way I am perceiving. Resist the temptation to modulate your experience. Instead, find that thing in yourself which is creating the experience. **In the middle of a dream, find the dreamer. In the middle of life, find the being.**

It is a question of hunting yourself. It is a question of going deep into that who perceives, into that who exists. After a while, it'll dawn on you that whatever realization you're having about yourself, whatever experience you are concocting about yourself, is also a dream about yourself. Whether you experience sorrow, suffering, happiness, enlightenment or liberation, all you can experience is a dream. Even the hunting for yourself, even the stalking of yourself, even the finding of yourself and the mastery of yourself is a dream.

There is nothing but the Self surrounded by an infinite extension of light—nothingness unexperienced, new, unborn.

The key of dreaming is the key of existence: the mastery of perception.

Find the dreamer. Search for the manner in which you create the dream. Know yourself standing in a vast field of light in infinite extension without any identity, without any name, without any experience; knowing fully well that whatever dream you seem to be having, whatever life you seem to be living, you are only recreating the shadow of your dealings with light. You are nothing but the interpreter between your perception and the light. Every dream and every experience is an act of interpretation. How you think of it, how you perceive it, how you react to it, is the key to master your dream. If you jump into trying to change the dream, you're going to miss the fact that you are already producing a dream, and this dream you're producing gives you tremendous data. This is the dream that you have created. Search for the center of that dream. Understand how you are dealing with the vast light. Whether you dream a dream of rich experience, or you just dream with a rock, or the dream of darkness, the dream of desperation, the dream of separation, the dream of love or the dream of enlightenment... whatever dream you're dreaming, use it, see it, touch it. Know that you are creating it and ask yourself: "How am I creating this?" Don't answer yourself with the mind. That's just dreaming of language. Instead, touch it, hear it, feel it—not tomorrow, not next week, just now. Feel it. See it. Smell it. Understand that all these experiences are just your dealings with light.

When you find it, you will realize that it's always been *you* dreaming; that the entire universe is the dream of one being and one being only; that you have been sleeping and waking within a dream, and never truly fully awake because there's nothing outside of yourself; that you have been dreaming dreams of life and death, of evolution, of reincarnation, of gods and devils and wars, a dream of revolution and liberation; that you have been dreaming all this time; and that there is nothing but layers of dreams.

The only thing beyond the Dreaming itself is the pure, unblemished nothingness—just the silent sound of the eternal.

Your dealing with this eternal void creates reverberations of shadows and experience. That is all you have been experiencing. There has never been any other dreamer. There has never been, ever, any other dreamer. It does not matter how you change or modify the illusion; what always remains is the fact that you are the master of your perception, and you can't avoid the truth about the matter.

The Other Self

When you are born, so that your physical body can have a form, a creature of light and shadow is fused to your body—an energy form with its own thoughts, feelings, likes, and dislikes. It goes everywhere you go. It moves when you move. As soon as you are born, it takes the shape of your body. If you move your hand, its hand moves with you. If you cry, it experiences the crying. If you speak, it moves its mouth. It hears the sound of your voice. It feels the vibration of sound and air running through your chest. It is present in every micro-expression of your face, every twitch of every muscle. It is there, in bed, when you sleep, when you dream. It tosses around when you toss around. And everyone who addresses you, addresses it. It hears all. It sees all that you see. It hears your thoughts, the most intimate ones. It has been where you have been, and what you touch, it touches. When you suffer, it feels the pain. In this creature of light and shadow, everything that you experience and do and witness is recorded. It is impregnated with the entire experience of this lifetime since the moment you are born. It is the Other Self. But just like it hears your thoughts and moves as you move, it also thinks its own thoughts. It has its own wants, its own likes and dislikes, and just as it hears your thoughts, you hear its thoughts. Every thought that comes from the Other Self, you hear it as if in your own voice. You hear it inside as a whisper.

It can tell you to do things; it can advise you to go here and not to go there. It might tell you to take a rope, hang it on a beam in your house and hang yourself. It might whisper in your head that your life is worthless, that it'd be better if you were dead, that the suffering is too much. It might ask you...induce you, trick you into drinking, into faltering to your oaths and promises. It might guide you to buried treasure. It might guide you to an esoteric school and a Teaching. It might bring you to the heights of spiritual attainment or it might drag you down to the worst hellish nightmare. Each time you hear the thoughts of the Other Self, you hear them as if they were your own.

The secret of the Other Self is that it's made up of astral light, keen to emotional shifts and disturbances, impressionable by creatures unseen and of magick.

The Other Self is the Dream Self itself.

As your body lays in bed and your conscious grasp of your form dissolves into that dreamless state of the in- between, the Other Self can separate a little bit from you. Although retaining your form and, somewhat, your identity, it moves about in the dream lands. It goes to have experiences that you can't always have in a physical body. It moves. It speaks. It thinks. And as it moves and speaks and thinks, you sleep. You wake up with the memory of having done and spoken and thought. You say you dreamt yourself in this room, with these people. You say, "I had a dream," and the dream you had was the experiences of the Other Self.

The dreams you have are the life of the Other Self; but you are inseparable from your Dream Self, even as it goes into its own world and adventure and you lay in bed in your organic body. The organic body is dreaming the Dream Self. Nothing happens to the Dream Self. It can't be killed. It can't be harmed (not mostly—sometimes, but not mostly). For, when the dream is over and the dream land disappears, all light—which is a projection of the encounter of yourself with the Beast—simply retreats into the shape that you're given in this lifetime. Then, you wake up and you go about your day, and you go and you speak and you think. As you go and speak and think, your Dream Self goes, speaks, and thinks. In this sense, it is said that you dream your Dream Self and your Dream Self dreams you. Your life is the dream of the Other Self, just as your dreams are the life of the Other Self.

Thus, when something happens to your body, any suffering, and even the ending of life itself, it does not really harm the Other Self. For, whatever form it takes, your consciousness simply goes back into the land of the Dreaming and the Other awakens as you awaken. The Other Self is with you *now*. The Other Self is listening to every word, to every hum, to every creak and slush. It hears every whisper of your thoughts. It takes the shape of your hand and your shoulders, your head. It looks where your eyes look. It is here, reading these words. As you read this, my Dream Self speaks through me from the dream lands, communicating from Dream Self to Dream Self while the organic body is passive, rested, in slumber, receiving all impressions.

There are moments (are there not?) when we dream and we do things in that dream that makes us think, *I would simply not do that in waking life*. Yet, there we are, doing them in the dream lands. "That was not me," you may say. "It's the Dream Self. "Yet there are times in our daily life, in our waking state, when we enter a state of as-if-asleep, and the Dream Self takes over and does things you don't remember doing. Those things you "would not do" when you're awake.

Don't you see that the same thing happens in those rare moments when you are dreaming and you become lucid? That's a moment when your waking self takes over the dream body. Then you do things that the dream body would not do. You move through the

Dream Self and then you think through the Dream Self. You direct it and you live the dream of the Dream Self.

There is another side to that coin; there is another side to being lucid in a dream. It is when the Dream Self is lucid in your daily life, and then the Dream Self feels the rush of blood in this body and the electrical currents of electricity running through its entire being. It can see through your eyes. It can experience a moment of organic life, and it can take over the actions and decisions of this self. The counterpart of the lucid dreaming is the unconscious waking, when you're no longer in control of your experience, when you gave it all to the Dream Self. It may have mischievously placed your keys where you knew you didn't leave them or said words that you don't remember saying. Or, maybe, it has been in control entire days and weeks without you being present. Be careful with an entirely lucid dreaming. Without the participation of the Other Self, that simply means the Other Self was unconscious in its own life. Be careful not to get into a war with your own self. Do not try to eliminate it; you must know it, control it. You must impregnate upon it the desire to achieve the purpose of your incarnation so that it may guide you to hidden treasures, through adventures and dungeons; so that it might bring you to the chambers you need to visit; so it may connect you to the people you need to know. A partnership, such as the partnership of a man and his horse, is needed—a joint experience of all the Self goes through.

With enough mastery over the Other Self, you learn to move about in the Dreaming as you will. You create a vessel, a form. You inhabit this vessel and this form created with the body of the Other Self. You place your consciousness in this vessel of *dream stuff* and you move about in the other realms and other worlds. You move up in levels, up to the spirit world and the astral world and the etheric world, up to the mental plane and the Buddhic plane and higher up into planes beyond description. Until you are capable of tremendous feats of wonder in the dream, so you may also, if such is your lot, bring the Dream Self into the waking and move about as if in a dream and become shadow, become invisible and move through walls and glide and grow as you will, or disappear. For everything that is possible in a dream is also possible in the waking, as long as you have the right vessel for it.

The danger of this dual existence is when your will is divided in two, and what you will is not what the Other Self wants. You have failed to bring the Other Self into conformity with your True Will. Then, there is a tug-of-war in the lifetime. But, if you manage to control this and create a union between the two, all manners of experience and all manners of knowledge are possible for you. Then, what it does, you know; and, what you do, it knows. All goes back to being the way it was before there was any separation between the Dream Self and your waking self. If it manages to awaken when you are awake, if it becomes lucid without you going to sleep, then you both hear, listen, and concur in single-minded action; then your waking life becomes your dream life. You sit with people. You move. You go to work. You drive your car and you dream, and the dream is as vivid and as clear as the Sun at High Noon. It is as light, as sound, as crisp and clear as the world. But you live in two places at once, and you might be discombobulated, not knowing if you are here or there. Or, you may realize that you were just off somewhere else doing something else in a different place. What you did there seemed just as real and as clear as your present surroundings. And the same thing might happen in a dream, where you are sure that you are awake, yet it is a dream. Or you are awake; and you believe yourself to be dreaming because of the movements of the astral waters, the shadows, the weird things about. For a moment, it's disconcerting not knowing where you are and who you are. If you go beyond this, there is unity, power, and clarity. If you freak out at this point, you will seek to go back to a place with no power, with no dreaming. You will seek the ordinary, and you will seek to hold on to your ordinary life and never let go.

To master the Dreaming is to be a conscious warrior while waking and while dreaming. It is to know, to communicate and to subjugate both selves to the will of your True Self—which is not two but one. For, whether we sleep or wake, any experience is a dream being had by the Highest. Any experience that you may seem to be having is still part of the dream— whether waking or sleeping, it is still a dream. The voyager, the silent center of light without dimensions, is always perceiving, always dreaming. That observer is not divided. It's neither of the dreaming nor of the waking, but from above. Only that can master the waking and the dreaming. Search, then, for the True Self. There is the key to mastery. There, in that mastery, is the key to the Dreaming and, in the Dreaming, is the key of existence.

The Golden Flower

When a word is uttered, there is a moment of silence before the word and a moment of silence after the word. Between a silence and a silence, there is something born. Something moves through. Something dies. Just so, before a lifetime and after a lifetime, there is an ocean of silence. The lifetime is just an island existing in between a sleep and a sleep. So a dream, any dream, exists as an island in between a sleep and a sleep. It makes little sense to ask for a longer duration, because every lifetime, just like every dream, lasts exactly as long as it is. Every lifetime has a beginning, a middle, and an end. Such is the duration of every lifetime. From the perspective of the eternal, we do not count in minutes, years or aeons. We count beginnings, middles and ends. Surrounding the island of experience there is the vast ocean of the unknown. Just as the beginning of a word is a mystery and its ending an unknown, so the beginning of a life is a forgetfulness and its ending a mystery. So begins every dream after a moment of not being. After the dream, another silence.

But what is this space that holds consciousness? What is this space, this island of experience? What is holding that? In a way, it is not a sequence in time. The sequence in time is what we experience as we are moving through this island of consciousness, but from the perspective of the eternal, it is all happening at once. One moment of experience does not follow another in a sequential line. Instead, it opens like the petals of a flower. Every moment of existence and every moment of the dream opens and unfolds out of itself. From the perspective of the eternal there is no middle, beginning and end. There is an unfolding, always happening in the same place. For those of us who live in the non-dreaming, in the lands without occurrence and without experience, we see the island of the Tonal—

117

this moment of experience called dream, lifetime, word, story—as a flower. This flower is a special kind of flower, growing in this garden of dark eternity. It is a flower with a specific color, with a unique scent and with an unmistakable sound. The color of the flower is golden. It starts with a tiny speck, a dot, a tiny impurity in the vastness of silent dark—just like the light of a star in the infinite night. It begins with that tiny, little golden light and it flowers open—its petals moving away from the center.

If you look within with a silent mind and do not get carried away with the contents of your thoughts, and do not get carried away with the quality of your experience—if you're able to look at any experience, any lifetime, any dream from the outside, from that tower of eternity—you might come to see this golden flower. Moving or static, it does not matter; but yellow its color. If you look closely at this flower, whose aroma is thunderous like the reverberation that creates the universe, you will see the hue of its color. You will see the texture of its petals. If you are able to see the yellow flower of the Dreaming, you will have the secret behind the Dreaming. It is now here, in front. It is permeating the space, this golden rose, its yellow petals everywhere in the space. It is in its texture. Its movement and its ripples cause a disturbance in the silence of the mind, giving the illusion of something happening. For, as you well know, any dream is an imperfection of sleep, just like mind is an imperfection of consciousness.

The yellow rose, with its golden petals, contains the totality of the Dreaming. It contains every possibility of experience. It can only be seen from above, from the eternal landscape of the dark, from that place that has no I, no movement, and no mind. Its first and only impression is the yellow rose with its unique petals, its unique aroma of thunderous creation, its sound of all- pervading hum.

To successfully enter the secret behind the Dreaming, look for the yellow rose. See it in your mind. Open. Open the gates at the top of your head and allow its petals to unfold its golden light, to flow down and to fill your consciousness with the seeing of the rose and its petals. Once you see it, you will know it. Once you know it, you'll know the secret behind the Dreaming. Once you obtain the vision of the yellow rose, all manners of experience—whether a lifetime or a dream—are fully accessible to your consciousness.

I am telling this to you exactly as it is. There is no metaphor, no trickery, no image behind these words. See the yellow golden light in its unfolding petals. See the rose of the Dreaming. If you see it, it's yours.

Every word that I tell you now emanates from this yellow rose. Every word is born, exists and dies as the unfolding of this rose. There is no one telling you this story. It unfolds. It tells itself. It is heard, lived and experienced. Then it's gone and it dies, and the only one to see it is one *I*, one observer without perspective, without changes, without a name—just a single point of observation in the vast night of eternity. This *I* sees the yellow rose, obtains the vision of its golden petals and knows itself as the center of the rose, as the one point of consciousness in the vast ocean of eternity. It knows itself as the center of the rose, and it knows the rose to be truly the one vision of its own surroundings. And, thus, the dream begins and unfolds and moves and dies and is reborn in a never-ending unfolding of experience. Thus, the island of the Tonal and, thus, the life and, thus, the dream comes and goes, and it never, ever, ends because it was never here, because it was never somewhere else; because it is, at its center, I, and in its circumference, the vast.

The Going

Sometimes, I wonder just how long I have been here. Sitting here in this space, with the smells of incense and smoke. The burning candle of honey-sweet. How long I've really been behind this curtain of light, surrounded by darkness all around. Just how long have these violet lights been staring at me like the two unlikely eyes of an enormous beast? How long has the aroma of coffee and burning lights been reaching up to my nostrils? It wasn't that long ago, I don't think, that my eyes were closed and the world did not exist. Not long ago, I think, that no thought was crossing the landscape of consciousness. No mind was disturbed by no one. Since no event happened after any other event, a moment in eternity is both endless and instantaneous. It took the slight disturbance—a calling, a naming—for me to open my eyes and see the smoky light before me. Silhouettes of shadows.

Since I find myself here and I perceive something watching me, I begin to sense around myself a body, a physical presence, something roughly made of form in time. Movement is felt—passing of light and shadows. After a while, I wonder if I've always been here, if I've always been wondering how long I've been here. I could name myself one-thousand and one names. I could cast myself out into one of the innumerable shadows that happen to appear before me in between that moment of silent non-existence.

That deep darkness I sense surrounds me. I can't really perceive that darkness—more like a feeling at the edge of my sensing. Though, I must confess, I do see darkness all throughout, touching everything. But, how true can that darkness be if I can see it? A play, a shadow of light and sound is truly what I perceive. This shadow play is neither the blinding light of pure consciousness nor the dark abyss of silent death. This experience seems endless. For, no matter how many times I seem to dissolve myself, I keep coming back to this moment, to this space where I seem to be experiencing something. Yet, nothing seems to ever be happening to me. I am, therefore, in the midst of the Dreaming. I am the dreamer who realizes he is but a speck of imagination, a tiny particle of dust in the mind of an eternal sleeper; that He Who Sleeps, the God who slumbers is, for a tiny moment, *almost* waking up, and in waking up gives birth to me and to this palace of its creation. I find myself going in between spaces, moving around. Even if I seem to be statically sitting in one place, one moment after another keeps moving, propelling, me forward. I am always moving from instant to instant, from dream to dream. I know I am not as real as He who is no-man and does not awake and does not think and does not experience and does not know. It simply absorbs all that is. I know I am not as real as That which is not. Yet, I am the Going. And from here to there, my consciousness threads this experience to that, this moment to the next. I am the Going. I am the dream eater. I am perception. I am the center of my experience. I am dreamer. I am the dream. I am the light and the darkness. I am the shadow-play. Projection of darkness, projection of light—a smoky mirror is what I am. I am the Going. I move in the vast ocean surrounded by a bubble of shadow. I am the Going. I fall and I move. I fall and I return. Never static, never in one place. Always not here, for as soon as I think I'm about to see myself, I am gone. I look for myself and I am no longer there. Speck of shadow. I am the Going.

The silent darkness permeates and penetrates every particle of existence, and through the darkness of eternal now, bursts open the silent, blinding speech. Silence broken by silence. The dark silence broken apart by the silence in speech.

I have always been here. I, the dreamer, have existed from the beginning of time. I have experienced what every dreamer has ever experienced. What every man, god, animal or stone have perceived, I have dreamt. I have existed from the beginning of time until the end of time. I shall perdure and exist until the death of the last flame of the last star. Therefore, I am all men and I am no man. Therefore, I am the dreamer. Never in one place, I am the Going. Never observing the real, just shadows. Never the light, only projections of light. Never the darkness, only shadows of light. I am neither the light nor the darkness, for I am none and, therefore, all. I am the Going. I am dreamer.

The Three Keys

As a solar being—one of eternal wakefulness—one finds it hard to understand how to fall asleep, how to let go of this eternal brilliant consciousness that is not just something one has acquired. It's not just a limb, a vestment. It is this eternal wakefulness; not something one can simply discard, take off, obscure. For, it is the very nature of self. It is at the core of anything that one can be. **How, then, can a solar consciousness—a god who never sleeps—ever understand the dark repose, the embrace of the night?**

Understand, also, that the question of how to sleep is no different for such an entity than the question of how to die. How can the unborn eternal living God ever lay down his life? How to give up that which he never acquired: his life? How to give up that which he always was? Yet, to dream, to die, to incarnate, to be born, and to sleep, one needs to know both, how to die and how to sleep.

If a manual were to be written for such a god, for such an eternal, unchanging consciousness, one could, perhaps, take a look through the eternity of space and time, and look closely on that little girl dancing round and round and round on the wet grass, and her summer dress lifting up—yellow—lifting as she twirls. Tiny little Sufi girl swirling and twirling, arms extended up to the heavens. She looks up to the blue sky, which becomes a disk of luminous blue, and the Sun shines somewhere off the horizon, providing a horizon of light as round and as moving as the edges of her skirt. She swirls and twirls around; and if this god of eternal consciousness were to enter this little girl's soul and let himself be moved by her play, she would arrive at one point unknown to silence, but clear to the dancer—a point where, if she stops, the world moves and the magick of the

125

Goddess becomes evident. **For, as soon as she stops her dance, the entire universe revolves around her as a mad, mad whirlwind. It revolves around her and it takes away, in that magnificent swirl, her consciousness.**

The brilliance of her silent identity is syphoned-out by the momentum of the universe rotating around that center of gravity. In a swoon, the little girl follows suit and falls to the ground, arms open in eternal surrender or in tender embrace. At this point, the difference is unclear to us. But she lays down, and in that brief moment when identity and the center of consciousness is syphoned-out into the maelstrom of creation, the Goddess meets death. For a brief moment, she sleeps, and dreams.

Or, perhaps one could direct the attention of this god of eternal, unrelenting, undying consciousness to the soul of that little twelve-year-old boy who was captured just two hours ago in the house of his father and taken away, along with three other friends, by the security forces with orders to execute everyone in that house. The little boy of twelve is kneeling next to an open grave. One of his friends is already resting in the grave. The little twelve-year-old boy is kneeling, looking at his future: that calm, restful corpse who used to be his playmate, who used to laugh like a train whistles, who used to play pranks, who used to sing and dance, who used to like to climb trees and fall, who had that unique heat to his body. Now, he emitted no heat, no laughter, no sound, no play. Yet, he emits something. **He emits an extremely subtle, light, almost cold touch—almost like the spray of mist the orange emits when cut by the knife. The sensation of that spray on the face touching as a caress that almost did not happen. This breath emanating from the body of the corpse is so subtle that it cannot be clearly perceived by the senses.** Yet, it is clearly perceived by the solar plexus. With the impression of this emanation, the last breath of that corpse touches the heart of this little twelve-year-old boy about to be executed.

There is a soldier behind him, and the soldier is pointing his gun at the back of his head. The boy knows that he cannot escape this moment; that he cannot plead his way out; that he cannot be polite, bargain, convince, threaten or in any other act change the moment. All there is, is the cold touch of death in front and the harsh unknown presence behind. At that moment, if this god were to enter the seed, he would choose the source of power, as gods always do, and know that the power exists, in this moment, in the soul of the twelve-year-old boy. He would inhabit it. He would perceive the vastness of the void behind his back. **God would know that, in his eternal wakefulness, he's always been surrounded by this eternal, unmoving, untouchable abyss behind him. He would know the nature of death as this harsh unknown behind, as this cold emptiness, pregnant with all possibilities. He would then feel himself surrender to the moment, yet remain incredibly aware of the threat of death behind—the darkness of the void behind becoming as wings to the soul of this body.** No longer a threat, just an undeniable openness behind, he surrenders. He surrenders, not to what is happening to his body. He surrenders to the sensing of this open void behind his back. And in this manner, this god of eternal consciousness may come to see what we mortals face each night as we fall asleep and allow our consciousness to give itself up to that eternal dark embrace of sleep.

Or maybe he could come to the rooftop of a house and see this man who has ingested strange drugs, who is looking at the night sky and sees the valleys and mountains, the rivers and oceans of dark space above him. He comes to see the infinite emptiness of the night sky as a terrible, strange landscape that exists outside tangible matter—existing not solely within anyone's imagination. It is something that is clearly there, imperceptible, unfathomable, non-conceptualized, never touched, never seen, never conceived, yet clearly there. **Something in this man, who has ingested strange drugs, can touch this vastness of emptiness. Were this god of eternal consciousness to enter the soul of this man, he would come to open his eyes and see home. In seeing home, he would feel as if he's looking in a mirror, being pulled into his own image. This man, lying on the rooftop of his house, would find his solar plexus being pulled up through this vacuum, like the tides of the ocean are pulled up by the silver moon. He's going to feel like he's about to fall. He would grab with his fingernails the edges of the tiles, in his desperation for retaining the world he used to know, at the exact moment that he realizes the world will never be the same again. In this swift moment between *I am* and *I am not*, God knows his mirror image. In the switch, there comes death, his own negation.**

Through the levity into the empty void and its mirror image, the surrendering into the sinking-into-water, lies the key for moving between a dream and a dream, between an eternity and an experience. And there, in the perception of the void behind one's back, is the power to know one's Self and to forget one's self. And there, in the swirling and the syphoning-out of the center of experience, is the key between absolute power and absolute surrender. In those three keys, any experience can be obtained, every dream accessed, and every state of consciousness conquered.

Appendix

Kabbalistic Analysis of the Dreaming

Full Moon through the door.
Like a camel through the eye
of arcane needle.

The Bible tells the story of a rich man who came to Jesus and asked him how to attain life eternal. Jesus tells him to live a good life by following the Ten Commandments. The rich man declares he already does that, but something is lacking. Jesus then tells him to sell all his possessions, give them to the poor, and follow him. The rich man goes away sad because he knows he won't be able to do this. Jesus declares two things of importance. One is that "it is easier for a camel to go through the eye of a needle than for a rich man to enter the Kingdom of Heaven." And two is that, to do what he is asking the rich man to do is impossible for a man, because this transformation is only possible for God.

While most people interpret this passage as either an admonition against greed or as a justification for tithing, the esoteric import goes in a quite different direction. The rich man is complaining that, while his external life is in observation of religious duty, he is not yet complete. Jesus' answer seems to imply that the existing moral code, the Ten Commandments, should be but a stepping stone to get the man into an abundant and rich life. However, when the rich man asks what he still lacks, Jesus does not give him another code, but simply tells him to let go of something so that completion or perfection can emerge. What most people miss is the fact that the rich man cannot give up his wealth, not because he doesn't want to, but because only God can produce the type of transformation necessary to let go of what holds him back. If we take the man's wealth to be a symbol for one's accumulated experience, the totality

131

of one's identification with organic life, we can then begin to see the story's full import.

Now, let's take a look at the meaning behind these terms. The Hebrew for *rich* and *abundant* is *ashir* (Ayin- Shin-Yod-Resh), with a value of 580 in gematria. This is what the man had, yet he is unsatisfied with his mere material success and looks for the sense of profound peace and spiritual completion known as shalom (with a numerical value of 376). To go from *ashir to shalom*, you extract the difference: 580 - 376 = 204. The value of *Bara* is 204, which means *Son, or Son of God*. Therefore, the ending remarks of Jesus when he claims that to do this transformation is impossible for a man[1] but possible for God, he is passing on the formula of this transformation. To do this, however, divine intervention is needed. This divine intervention comes through the seed of God. When the rich man walks away, he is sad because he knows he cannot do this. Exoteric interpretation of the text leads most people to infer that the man is simply greedy. Jesus' commentary, however, makes it clear that it is impossible for an ordinary person to accomplish what he asks. God is needed.

The esoteric import of this parable is given in the adage: "It is easier for a camel to pass through the eye of a needle than for a rich man to enter the Kingdom of Heaven. "This adage gives the formula by which God's help is invoked. *The eye of the needle* refers to the path of Qoph,[2] and the camel to the path of Gimel,[3] in the Tree of Life.

---

1 Impossible, that is, to a *man of the world*—which is a man stuck in the material possessions of the sphere of Malkuth, the 10th sephira or emanation of the Tree of Life.

2 *Qoph* is the 19th letter of the Hebrew alphabet. It means *back of the head*, but it is often called "the eye of the needle "because of the shape of the letter.

3 *Camel* in Hebrew. The letter Gimel is written with a Vav and a Yod at its base. It is a symbol often associated in the ancient world with a rich man running after a poor man (symbolized by the subsequent letter, Daleth) to give him charity.

This passage reflects the Essene teachings by stating that these two paths are connected. Of course, both are ruled by the moon and both are connections between two different triads.[4] Qoph connects Malkuth to Netzach, and Gimel connects Tiphareth to Kether. The former accounts for the connection between Manipura Chakra and our organic body, while the latter shows how the dewdrops of Amrit descend from the back of the head when the ojas are activated by the interaction of Ajna with Vishudda, activating the sacred fluid in the cerebellum.[5]   The biblical passage is telling us how the interaction between these two passages is a key to the alchemical transformation. Let us examine each passage briefly and see how they interact alchemically.

In the microcosmos, the path of Qoph connects Manipura with the body. Since the path of Qoph is associated with both the moon and the back of the head, it is the path responsible for dreaming. Jodorowsky, Jung, Campbell and others see dreams as the archetypal language used by the body to communicate with the mind. These images are the oneiric language of the unconscious. Their origin can be just the subconscious mind trying to catalogue and make sense of the raw impressions of that day, or even a registry of current imbalances or impressions on the body. Of course, this path can bypass the conscious mind, and the impressions coming through are not necessarily of a logical nature nor voluntary. They are the dealings between the body and the soul.

---

4 The path of Qoph connects the third triad of the A.'.A.'., the man of Earth, with the *Lover* (the second triad of this order). The path of Gimel connects the Lover triad to the *Hermit* triad (the first triad of the order). This is because of the spheres that these paths connect on the Tree of Life.
5 This alchemical process is taught in various esoteric teachings of the East, and refers to substance that descends from the pineal gland, transforming the body and the mind

On the other hand, the channel can also carry signals from Netzach to Malkuth. Netzach can receive currents from Hod, Yesod, Malkuth and Tiphereth. Those signals coming from Yesod and Hod can affect our dreaming, of course, with both mental and erotic imagery, but they also open up the possibility of acquiring a conscious relationship with the Dreaming under intent. More importantly, these paths offer the possibility of transforming Qoph from a channel to the subconscious, to a channel to the divine, and the ability to make of the body a temple for God through the *arte alchemica*. When the path of Qoph is dormant, it serves as the channel for unconscious communication between body and soul. In "The Wake World,"[6] the bride describes her encounter with Qoph as follows: "There were nasty Jackals about, they made such a noise, and at the end I could see two towers. Then there was the queerest moon you ever saw, only a quarter full."[7]   When the moon is waxing, the dreaming is ruled by shadows, phantoms, and chaotic dualistic fluidity. The jackals, of course, are a reference to Anubis in his dual form of Anpu (who opens the road to the land of the subconscious and the underworld) and Ap-uat (who opens the road to the heavens). Anubis, therefore, serves as the guide who takes us through death and sleep, either to the subconscious or to heaven. The two towers they guard signify the path of Peh,[8]   and its tower, which is the House of God, is here presented in its duality. Either way, Kephra will bring the sun through to its dawn, whether through the subconscious lands of the dreaming or through the Bardos[9] between incarnations. The sun

---

6 Crowley, Aleister. *Konx Om Pax.* I highly recommend this story, "The Wake World," for an enlightening Kabbalistic account of the Dreaming as an allegorical passage of the dormant human soul through the Tree Of Life towards its awakening.

7 *ibid*, pg 9

8 17th letter of the Hebrew alphabet. It means *mouth*. In the Tree of Life it is connected with Trump XVI, The Tower.

9 The Western tradition popularly recognizes three transitional states of ex istence: birth, life, and death. The Tibetan tradition recognizes a fourth state, the in-between state called the *Bardo*. For an enlightened rendition of this state in the Western World, see *American Book of the Dead*, by E.J.

comes up just as sure as we wake up once again or are reincarnated after the passage of death. However, the passage through this land offers the opportunity of a different kind of rebirth. The key is in the unification of all dualities under intent. This rebirth, as the parable of the rich man suggests, is only possible for God. The sun, of course, is not dead but shining its light on the moon.[10] If the moon is full through this passage, it will reflect the light of the sun and the passage is guided by intent. If Netzach contains the light of Tiphareth, the moon of Qoph will fill up with the light of divine intent and love. Another way to express this principle is to say that, if the Fool (Atu 0), being the only thing that survives the destruction of The Tower (Atu XVI), safely attaches to Netzach, then the path of Qoph will activate and unify soul and body under will. The path of Gimel is associated with the full moon. This path connects the Sahasrara Chakra with Anahata Chakra through Sushuma Nadi. It carries the kundalini up to the crown during Dhyana, as well as the Amrit[11] down to the lower chakras, activating them. In the macrocosmos, this is the passage through which the Holy Guardian Angel descends after the union between Chokmah and Binah opens the door of Daleth and gives birth to the Son. In a sense, Qoph connects the body directly with Manipura, just as in the macrocosmos the Earth and its biosphere are directly connected, albeit controlled by the passage and tides of the moon. But the path becomes active only when the moon has become full with the light of the sun. In other words, while the forces of Manipura are always in contact with our body, the path becomes fully active and conscious through Dhyana.[12] Through Dhyana, the solar current Gold.

10 The scene described in "The Wake World" is also depicted in the 18th trump card (Atu XVIII), The Moon, of Crowley's Thoth tarot.

11 This is the alchemical sacred substance that transforms ordinary consciousness into divine consciousness. It is the elixir of ecstasy and the healing nectar of the gods.

12 *Dhyana* is one of the eight limbs of yoga, and it's characterized by the mind in a state of silence, illumination, and communion with the true nature of the higher Self.

lluminates the dark passages of our subconscious and allow body and soul to carry through the will of our spirit. Dhyana resolves the duality and shadows of the subconscious by unification and dissolution, and just like The Fool, survives the destruction of The Tower, the solar will survives the passage through the night. Let us examine how exactly the activation of Qoph[13] takes place. The kundalini serpent awakens in Muladhara and ascends to Swaddishtana. In one who is a slave to the sleeping state, this energy will follow the path of wants and organic tendencies. From the point of view of the mind, thoughts that flow and attach themselves to wants, fears, and mechanical tendencies give life to phantoms, *kleshas*,[14] and illusions. These mechanical thoughts tend to feed the libido and ground themselves in Malkuth through organic, automatic orgasm. A magician, however, learns to send the Kundalini and thoughts through the path of Peh, raising the energy towards Manipura, instead of grounding it. Once in Manipura, the seed planted there finds itself in Netzach, which, since it is at the bottom of the right hand pillar of the Tree Of Life, is pulled up towards the upper branches of the Tree. However, the vibration which connects to Netzach must be in alignment with this sphere or it will be ejected. This point is important, because the thought which leaves Hod[15] does not arrive intact. The Tower is destroyed, and what survives either ascends towards Netzach or is dispersed in Malkuth. This principle points to a fallacy common to those who think that to practice sex magick, all they have to do is think at the moment of orgasm, and what they think will come true. In a sense, they are correct because all thoughts and words give birth

---

13 *Qoph* is the Hebrew letter that means "eye of the needle," and it represents the passage in the Tree of Life that connects the physical body (Malkuth) with the intuition and source of emotions (Netzach). Qoph is the wire in the psychic body of humans that is responsible for dreaming. The activation of this wire implies the attainment of lucidity and the infusion of the dream with the sacred light of God.

14 Attachments or unconscious habits.

15 Hod is the sphere that controls thoughts.

to an *astral child*,[16] but what results of that is not necessarily as the would-be magician imagines. They forget that the conscious word or image they hold will be dissolved once death (orgasm) overcomes the Tower. What remains, however, is the essence of the eidolon held by the intent of the magician.

Now, in works of lesser magick, the magician can send a seed prayer towards Netzach and, if he succeeds and it is in agreement with the Fates (the Wheel of Fortune), it will ascend as a prayer. The adept who is able to receive Gnosis through the paths of Mem and Ayin (from the waters of Binah and the will of his Sun) can, in turn, send it to Netzach by preparing an adequate vehicle (eidolon or thought form) which will carry his intent. This sacred intent is Bhakti Yoga. It is the type of thought that connects itself to a deity, higher aspiration, or sacred principle. If successful, the intent will lodge itself to the Venusian vibration of Netzach, and naturally ascend. At the same time, this seed of Will constitutes the solar influence which fills the Moon of Qoph with the light of our Sun. As a result, the dream world is now of a different quality. It carries that quality of sacred import. It is not so much the propensity to lucidity, but the atmosphere of a sacred chamber, and the kind of message from the dreaming, that has the touch of spawned genius.

The Greek word for truth is *alethia*, which refers to the awakening of the memory of truth. In Hebrew, the word for truth is *Emet* (Aleph-Mem-Tau), but if we transpose the letters we can obtain Mem-Aleph-Tau, which means *from within*, as the concept of truth in Greek also implies. The reader will remember that in the first paragraph we discussed how Bara, the Son of God, is what's extracted when the rich man gives his wealth (Ashir) to attain completion (Shalom). Bara also means *a well*. In a sense, the Son has a mystical equivalent

---

16 That is, a program in the astral plane that seeks its fulfillment by becoming real in Malkuth.

to the well, just as the *Phallus* and the *Kteis*[17]are equivalent in a complementary sense.

According to Crowley's *Liber 231*, the Fool abides between Asar and Asi, before embarking in his cosmic voyage. This book describes the passage of The Fool through creation, where eventually he comes to destroy and survive the ruins of The Tower; the Holly Virgin (the moon of Qoph) appears after this, transformed. This is the full moon, who is now the Holly Virgin, but used to appear as a scary woman with blood in her teeth. She is now a "fluidic fire" which uses a "thunderbolt"—obvious allusions to the kundalini that now rises up from Swaddhistana to Manipura. At this point, the moon invokes "the Scarab, the Lord Kheph-Ra, so that the waters were cloven and the illusion of the powers was destroyed."This parting of the waters is reminiscent of the parting of the waters in Genesis, before the creation of the universe. In this case, the sun comes out victorious: "Then the sun did appear unclouded, and the mouth of Asi was on the mouth of Asar."[18]

Kephra is what the full moon invokes so that the sun can pass through and emerge unclouded. This is what happens in the path of Qoph when intent is applied through the combination of desire with the love characteristic of Bhakti Yoga.[19]   Notice how the path of Resh shows how the "mouth of Asi was on the mouth of Asar." In the beginning, the Fool resided in joy between Asi and Asar. Now, with the emergence of the Will and its successful passage, these two kiss. The kiss is the ecstasy of union of that which was separated through duality. The redeemer, the Fool, emerges after this process and provides the union now in joy and ecstasy.[20]

---

17 Or, the penis and the vagina.
18 *Liber Arcanorum sub figura CCXXXI.*
19 The Yoga of Devotion, or divine love.
20 See *Liber 231.*

Within the confines of my own temple, I've noticed that when the energy moves up from Swaddhistana as a "fluidic fire" and, if the adoration and love towards the sacred eidolon has been kept without disturbance or distraction, there is a bolt of energy, like a light or thunderbolt, that moves from the third eye to the back of the head as I'm drifting into sleep. Without implying or assuming that this is an universal experience or, even, what the text of *Liber CCXXXI* signifies, it has provided an intimate landmark for the success of the operation within my own body. I know that the same feeling in Hod would, but for an internal tweak of intent and attention, produce the orgasmic release of semen outside the temple. What follows after this is not part of the conscious mind. Intent is present, yes, but not shrouded by thought or wakeful memory.

Qoph is treated in chapter 18 of Aleister Crowley's *The Book of Lies*, "On Dewdrops." While the death mentioned in that chapter is often related to orgasm, it should be more properly understood as *Samadhi*.[21] However, death is also the passage from wakefulness into sleep. This is why it is Anubis who guards the narrow passage between the towers in Atu XVIII; and this passage is a lower octave of Peh, which is a lower octave of Gimel. Indeed, in "The Wake World," the bride describes the path of Gimel as having a beautiful moonlike virgin who reads from a book. The idea of the practice, therefore, is not to hold on to a thought form as if the want is more important than the will. The thought, or word, which is used to propel the will across the void is to dissolve and be surrendered for the seed to survive. "The old life is no more" and what survives is "more He than all he calls He."[22] One is to let it go free, for one is not "its master, but the vehicle of it."[23] Crowley tells us to study this chapter along with chapters 1 and 16. These chapters address the casting of the Fool into the Night of Pan (N.O.X.). In the "Sabbath

---

21 The divine ecstasy of union and the ultimate goal of Yoga.
22 Crowley, Aleister. *The Book Of Lies*, "On Dewdrops".
23 *Ibid*

Of The Goat,"[24] the phallus is adored as explained in *De Natura Deorum*. "Liber Arcanorum" presents the Virgin of God (Daleth) as enthroned on a seashell and seeking "seventy to her four." Seventy is the path of Ayin (The Devil), which casts the seed of will into the mind and accounts for the love of union the Male experiences for the Female. The four is a door, Daleth, which opens the heaves and allows the Son to descend (the HGA and the Amrit). Now, Chapter 16 describes the path of Peh, and it is in this passage that The Tower is destroyed and, if done properly, the Fool makes his way across the Night Of Pan to be planted in Netzach.

While the Practicus of the A.'.A.'. needs to learn Chastity, the practice of the sexual magick of *De Natura Deorum* teaches the Practicus that Chastity is only one side of a triangle. Chastity, in yoga, is Dharana.[25] The ability to hold a thought without distraction is akin to the ability to hold the desire in a hard phallus without dissipating the force nor letting it go too soon. However, Dharana is not the telos, the end result. It is a necessary, yet not sufficient, part. Dharana is the discipline that can be accomplished in the left column of the Tree. There has to be a seed, a sacred aim, an aspiration. This is the second part of the triangle. Also, there has to be death. "Neither of these alone is enough." In the chapter "The Stag-Beetle" of *The Book Of Lies*, Crowley illustrates the path of Peh and, once again, shows how the three sides of the triangle are necessary. Here, Kephra is invoked by the moonlike Virgin of God. This process, where the adept merges with a deity by adoration throughout his lifetime (i.e., through the life of the phallus), and upon surrender during death, is the Love of Bhakti. This Love is essential for the activation of Qoph. The whole process of De Natura Deorum can be called Dhyana. Dharana, of course, is a necessary component, but the aim is Dhyana, or divine Love. However, one cannot, by the ordinary

---

24 *Ibid*
25 Holding one thought in the mind to the exclusion of any other impression, thought or emotion

will alone, bring about such result. All the lower ego can do is hold the seed with impeccability and surrender to death at the right moment. Going to sleep, after adoring the Phallus and its eidolon, without uttering the Word teaches the adept one third of another triangle (to be completed in a higher octave through the Third Step, or the secrets of the IXth degree of the OTO). Dharana can be done through the will of the lower ego, but as we know from Ashtanga Yoga, the aim is the destruction of the thought held in Dharana; and through the destruction emerges the divine contemplation of Dhyana, beyond ego and the conditioned mind. Dhyana is the divine result of the death of Dharana. As Jesus claims of the rich man, only God can do this. He tells the rich man to sell his possessions (i.e., having built his Dharana, cast himself unto the Night so that the kingdom of heaven can descend and make him whole). The results of this first practice are the activation of the back of the head (Qoph) and the subsequent emanation of the Amrit. This is the beginning of the reception of Gnosis, and the result is the first manifestations of spawned genius.

Most people are familiar with the phenomenon where someone goes to sleep with a pressing problem in mind and, if the issue has been held consistently for a long time in the mind, the dream will provide a solution, which is often described as *a stroke of genius*. The adept can use this principle consciously and with intent to climb up the mountain and activate the passages of his temple; but more importantly, to gain a connection with God that can guide his inner and outer life. When the rich man addresses Jesus, he explains that he follows the external law, his ethical code, impeccably. However, something is missing. His Yama practice is good, but the Niyama is not quite there. Crowley explains in *Liber ABA* that Niyama is best understood as *virtue*.[26] Yama is about the restrictions one places in one's life (the control of the square); but the circle one must follow

---

26 Crowley, Aleister. *Liber ABA*, chapter "Yama and Niyama."

is Niyama; which, in regard to one's external life, is the practice of one's talent, the manifestation of one's genius. The path of Qoph is connected to the practice of Niyama. It is through the flow of images and information from the subconscious that the artist, scientist, and innovator of any field draw the material that results in the works of genius that have the thumbprint of destiny. When one understands Qoph as related to Niyama, one can see that that spawned genius will result if the practice of the Adept is tied to his true will and not to mere wants. The Will comes from the Fool, and it is connected to one's Wheel of Fortune.[27]   The result of this practice will bring about works that are an execution of one's true will (Niyama). The Niyama and the Dhyana are similar principles, albeit in different levels. Niyama is the manifestation of one's genius, while Dhyana is the inner contact with the source of that light by the altar of the inner consciousness wherein which we seek Truth.

----

27 Atu X

About the Author

Koyote began his training among the volcanoes and jungles of El Salvador, where the revolutionary dreams of a just and good world framed his spiritual aspirations. While pursuing his Jesuit education and volunteering to create and lead a literacy program for the children of war refuges, Koyote trained in Tantra Yoga and Western Mysticism during his adolescence, until he was forced into exile when targeted by that troubled country's death squad.

In 1985 Koyote fled to the USA where he obtained political asylum and, eventually, his citizenship. He then took on the roll of householder and raised a family, worked full time, and pursued his graduate and post-graduate studies in Philosophy and Cognitive Sciences at UCSD and Santa Clara University. His worldly obligations did not stop his spiritual pursuits. He was initiated in Kriya Yoga and Magick while fulfilling his duties as a householder.

In 1995 he was initiated by his Yaqui-Lacandon benefactor into the Toltec tradition and the Path of the Infinite. Koyote was acknowledged as a teacher in the lineage by the elder Nahual, Teczaki Guitame Cachora.

He developed a Toltec improvisational performance art called The Telling, a mystical inducing experience known to affect and transform the listener through a direct and unmediated experience.

Koyote runs a branch of the A.'. A.'. under the Ox and None Clerk-House and Xicoco, an esoteric school of the Toltecs, where he trains students in magick, shamanism, mysticism, and yoga.

He has authored books and created seminars on the Yoga of Dreaming, meditation, astral voyaging, shadow walking, magick, the power of attention, alchemy, and tantra.

CONTACT INFORMATION

For information on courses and seminars taught by Koyote, as well as performances of The Telling, check out our website:
www.koyotetheblind.com

Check out Koyote's titles on his Amazon Author's Page:
www.amazon.com/author/koyote

Follow him on Facebook in "The Telling by Koyote the Blind" page:
www.facebook.com/koyotetheblind/

For further information on Gateways Consciousness Classics and a list of current publications, contact:

Gateways Books and Tapes
P.O. Box 370
Nevada City, CA 95959-0370
(USA)
www.gatewaysbooksandtapes.com
www.idhhb.com
email: info@gatewaysbooksandtapes.com
phone: (530) 271-2239 or
(in the U.S. and Canada) (800) 869-0658